Honolulu

Los Angel

2091 · · · 2228 ·

8276 MILES 4½ DAYS

Pago

COURSE OF THE
MATSON LINERS
IN THE SOUTH PACIFIC

TIKI STYLE

TiKi STYLE

A POCKET BIBLE VERSION OF
THE BOOK OF TIKI

by Sven A. Kirsten

TASCHEN

CONTENTS

A GUIDE FOR THE URBAN ARCHEOLOGIST

DISCOVERING A LOST CIVILIZATION IN YOUR OWN BACKYARD

"The wood-rot malady is spreading among the idols—
the fruit upon their altars is becoming
offensive—the temples need rethatching."
Herman Melville *TYPEE. A Peep at Polynesian Life*, 1844

These observations on the fate of the ancient Polynesian civilization from one of the classics of South Seas fiction seem strangely appropriate to describe the fate that has befallen the American Tiki style of the 50s and 60s. Its symbols, the Tikis, are decaying, the "Polynesian" cuisine of that period has become the antithesis of health food, and most of the surviving examples of Tiki architecture appear dilapidated.

But just as Paul Gauguin was fascinated with the melancholy atmosphere of decay in Papeete, Tahiti's capital, detecting "the blurred surface of some unfathomable enigma" in this already tainted paradise, so can today's Urban Archeologist appreciate remnants of that Paradise Lost of the American *dolce vita* we call Tiki style.

Tiki temples, once gracing every major American city, have vanished or been refurbished, the "uncouth jolly-looking images" (Melville) cast out with missionary zeal to make room for new gods (or styles). Waterfalls have ceased to flow like the mana (or the money) that built them, the Tiki torches have gone out, and outrigger beams been sawed off.

Yet the Urban Archaeologist has developed a sensitivity to lost cultures and their forgotten forms. He fearlessly travels to their sites in such remote and exotic places as Columbus, Ohio, or Pomona, in the urban sea of Los Angeles. For him, bobbing down some obscure freeway toward uncharted sub-suburbia on a smoggy day is as thrilling as steering the Kon-Tiki through a hurricane in the Pacific. Like an urban beachcomber, he sifts through the debris of consumer culture in thrift stores, yard sales, and used-book stores—in search of the artifacts and ephemera that provide pieces to the puzzle of the lost culture

that brought forth such concepts as that of the Urban Polynesian Paradise. With sense of wonder intact, the Urban Archeologist realizes that one does not always have to search far to explore the mysteries of forgotten ancient traditions, but that strange treasures can lie right in your own neighborhood, hidden under the layers of progress and development. It is our aim to nurture this ability to see the marvelous in the seemingly mundane through this book, your guide to Tiki culture in America.

First Palm in Calif 1769   2/19/20

IN THE BEGINNING ...

Ever since its fall from grace, humanity has yearned to find its way back to the paradise it was cast out of. When the first reports of the South Sea Isles reached the Old World, the tales seemingly described this lost haven. Polynesia became the metaphor for Eden on earth. But as the distant shores of the South Pacific were out of reach for most mortals, other mythical lands were sought out by the explorers.

One such place was "California," a mysterious island (it was believed to be a continent on its own) reputed to be endowed with Amazons and pearls. Even though once this *terra incognita* was settled and these flights of fancy proved to be an exaggeration, California has retained its status as a golden dream destination. Generation after generation arrived here, seeking to realize their own version of paradise. One such interpretation was the tropical garden of the South Sea Isles.

Thus the first palm tree was planted and tropical flora was propagated. And since not only the biosphere but also the psychosphere was present in California, a "Polynesia Americana" soon began to take shape. Tiki temples were erected, and for a while the people believed. They came to worship the cult of modern primitivism, naively engaging in such (now taboo) practices as alcoholism, racism, chauvinism, and pig-eating.

And as Californians emulated Polynesia, the rest of the nation looked to California for lifestyle guidance. Soon every major city in America was home to at least one Polynesian palace.

SKETCH

ΧΟΝΑ ΧΑΙ

RAIN FOREST

TAURANT

SHOPPES INC

DAVIS AIA ARCHITECT
THIRD ST. LOS ANGELES

TIKI-WHO WAS HE?

In the beginning was the word, and the word was: "TIK"!—at least according to renowned language archeologist and linguist Merrit Ruhlen of Palo Alto, California. He traced the origin of all human language back to this magic three letter word, surviving today as "toe," in the word *digit* (and obviously, *dick*). Endowed with such archetypal power, it is does not seem surprising that "Tiki" became the buzzword of a generation. But "Tiki" was not only close to the first word uttered by mankind: In Polynesian mythology; it is also the synonym for the first man. Looking the term up in A. W. Reed's *Concise Maori Dictionary*, one finds this expansion of the term:

1. TIKI: First man, or personification of man. Through ancestor worship this Maori Adam evolved into a half-god, and eventually "Tiki" was used as a term for all depictions of man, as we find in its next meaning:

2. TIKI: grotesque carving of a man decorating a house. A concise description of the kind of Tiki we find in these pages. But as we read on, the word reveals an even deeper significance:

3. TIKI: A phallic symbol. Indeed, in Maori lore, "Tiki" was the name for the procreative power and sexual organ of the god Tane, creator of the first woman. In the Austral Islands south of Tahiti, "Tiki-roa" (the long ancestral figure) was the nickname for the penis, and "Tiki-poto" (the short ancestral figure) endearingly designated the clitoris. For a word that holds such creative powers, it does not surprise us to find yet another meaning on the Marquesas Islands:

4. TIKI: God of the artists. To demonstrate that Tiki was indeed the muse of many artists, known and unknown, is one of the humble aspirations of this book. He seems to be perfectly suited to be the long needed protector of the artists.

ART FORMS OF THE PACIFIC AREA

COVARRUBIAS

PRIMITIVE ART IN
CIVILIZED PLACES

"Anyone who has ever seen them is thereafter
haunted as if by a feverish dream."
**Karl Woermann on Tikis in *Geschichte der Kunst
aller Zeiten und Völker*, 1900–1911**

The concept of using so-called "primitive" art to contrast and augment the
smooth lines of modern design has its origin in the inspiration the founding
fathers of modern art found in the seemingly naive and savage aesthetic.
When, in the early 20th century, more and more "artificial curiosities" (African
and Oceanic) made their way from the colonies to western European cities, a
young generation of artists, including Picasso, Miro, Klee, and Ernst, used the
inspiration they drew from primitivism to challenge the accepted concepts of
what art was. As Gauguin put it, studying the established classical arts "dis-
gusted and discouraged me, giving me a vague feeling of death without re-
birth."
Pablo Picasso underwent his seminal experience ("suddenly I realized why I
was a painter!") upon viewing the collection of primitiva at the Musée
d'Ethnographie du Trocadero in Paris. In fact, as early as 1919 he was hailed
as "an old adept of the Tiki." This was probably due to the fact that by around
1910 Picasso was the proud owner of a Marquesan Tiki that would later ac-
company him throughout the rest of his unparalleled career.
While primitive art was mainly appreciated by the avantgarde throughout the

20s and 30s, after the second World War it began, by virtue of this very association, to appeal to the affluent middle class: It was now associated with an artistic, bohemian lifestyle and a whimsical, playful attitude. By the late 1950s it was definitely de rigeur to have a striking tribal art piece to break the monotony of your contemporary living room decor. The time of the Tiki had come.

TRO

FRESNO

PICANA

CALIFORNIA

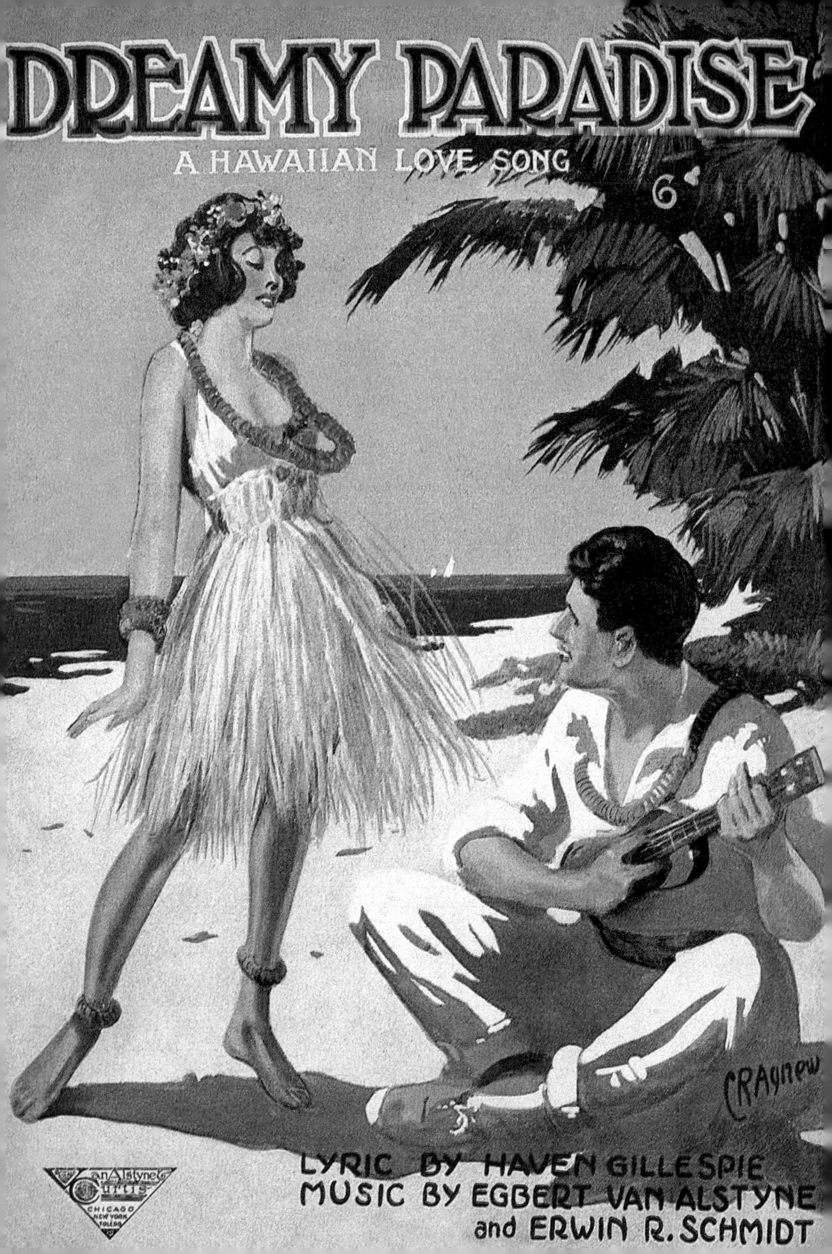
DREAMY PARADISE
A HAWAIIAN LOVE SONG
6
CRAgnew
LYRIC BY HAVEN GILLESPIE
MUSIC BY EGBERT VAN ALSTYNE
and ERWIN R. SCHMIDT
Van Alstyne & Curtis
CHICAGO NEW YORK TOLEDO

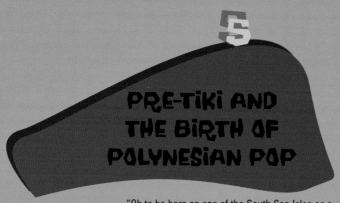

PRE-TIKI AND THE BIRTH OF POLYNESIAN POP

> "Oh to be born on one of the South Sea Isles as a
> so-called savage, for once to enjoy human existence
> as pure and untainted by a fake aftertaste."
> **Goethe, 1828**

The wish to forsake the benefits of civilization for a simpler, natural lifestyle is as old as "civilization" itself. Escapist dreamers and serious philosophers found that the early travelogues from the South Sea voyages of Cook and Bougainville described the perfect alternative living conditions in contrast to the affected society of Old Europe. Melville extolled the naturalness of the native girls: "I should like to have seen a gallery of coronation beauties, at Westminster Abbey, confronted by this band of Island girls; their stiffness, formality and affectation, contrasted with the artless vivacity and unconcealed natural graces of these savage maidens."

The fair climate, natural beauty, passionate natives, and abundant resources of exotic foods seemed to promise an existence free of the restraints and stresses created by the cultured communities of the Western world. In fact, adventure stories in the escapist vein set in Polynesia became so popular that in 1921 G. P. Putnam's Sons published a parody on such South Seas expeditions entitled *The Cruise of the Kawa*. The need for such fare was so great that although the book was clearly a satire by virtue of the photos alone it was accepted far and wide as a genuine narrative and its author was invited to speak in front of the National Geographic Society. The *Kawa* proved that fiction was preferable to fact when it came to renditions of paradise on earth. And it es-

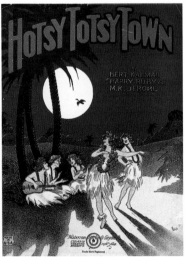

tablished the spirit of whimsy that from then on was to permeate Polynesian pop. But originally a much more archetypal instinct was addressed by the reports from Polynesia. "On the isle of Otaheite, where love is the principal occupation, the preferred luxury, or, more precisely, the unique luxury of the inhabitants, the bodies and souls of the women, are formed to perfection." (Joseph Banks, 1743–1820, naturalist on Captain Cook's *Endeavour*).

Statements like this transformed the nude native girl, the *wahine*, into the Eve in the Polynesian Garden of Eden. She became the first and foremost icon of Polynesian pop, embodying the promise of unconditional love. Soon other images like the palm tree, the native hut, the out-

rigger canoe, and all sorts of exotic flora and fauna joined her in the gallery of popular symbols of Oceanic culture. So far the Tiki was just one of many characters in the storybook land of Polynesia Americana.

The Hawaiian guitar made its appearance when the big Hawaiian music craze hit the mainland in the 1920s. Hawaiian entertainers became sought-after nightclub acts, and the clubs themselves began to emulate the tropical theme. Floor-to-ceiling bamboo and rattan, lush tropical plants, and murals of the Islands were the ingredients these early urban getaways used to create the illusion of having escaped to the South Seas. And soon the popular imagination focused on another image. Ever since the early European Zoos had begun to exhibit real live "wild men" as part of their displays and journalists were mocking the swooning reactions of the society ladies, the simultaneous attraction and repulsion felt towards the savage, the allure of the "exotic other", had entered the civilized consciousness of the Western world. In Polynesian Pop this fascination took the form of the heathen idol, the Tiki.

Aloha- Clifton's "Pacific Seas"
618 So. Olive St., Los Ange

PEOPLE YOU'RE APT TO MEET AT

SEE YOU AT THE Kahiki

POLYNESIAN SUPPER CLUB
3583 E. BROAD ST.

Arthur Godfrey

Zsa Zsa Gabor

Robert Goulet and Carol Lawrence

Andy Williams

Hugh O'Brian

Milton Berle

Edie Adams

Raymond Burr

Gig Young

Gordon and Sheila McRae

"The system of idolatry, which prevailed among a people separated from the majority of their species by trackless oceans, and possessing the means, not only of subsistence but of comfort, in an unusual degree, presents a most affecting exhibition of imbecility, absurdity, and degradation."
Rev. William Ellis, "Polynesian Researches," 1831

TiKi: RECREATIONAL LIFE-STYLE OF A GENERATION

By the 1950s Americans were ready to reap the rewards of the hard work that had brought them economic independence and affluence. They had emerged from the Second World War as heroes and were flying high on a cloud of international success and appreciation. But the same Puritan work ethic that had gotten them thus far also brought with it a whole package of traditional social and moral restrictions that were limiting their freedom to enjoy their prosperity.

Polynesian parties provided the outlet that allowed the man in the grey flannel suit to regress to a rule-free primitive naivety: Donning colorful aloha shirts (which did not have to be tucked in!), getting intoxicated by sweet exotic concoctions with names that resembled a lilting infant idiom (Lapu Lapu, Mauna Loa Puki), eating luau pig with bare hands, and engaging in hula and limbo contests provided the opportunity to cut loose and have fun in an otherwise conservative society. Another freedom that the "suburban savage" identity offered was that of beholding images of bare-breasted native women as long as it was in the context of anthropological interest – in other words, the practice of a sort of National Geographic eroticism. Thus the century-old myth of guilt-free sex was perpetuated, if not in action at least in the imagination. But as the

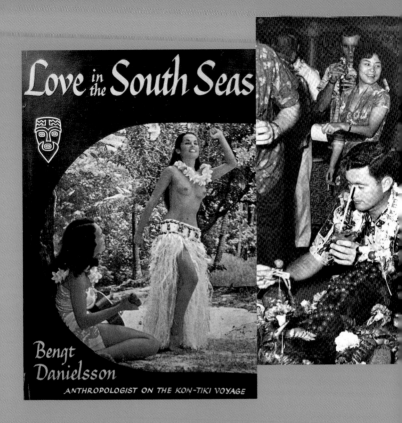

wahine and all the other clichéd icons of South Sea storybook-land were re-
cruited again, a new figurehead of Polynesian pop emerged: the carved native
idol commonly referred to as Tiki. Notwithstanding the fact that the term did
not exist in the Hawaiian or Tahitian languages, or that the stone sculptures of
Easter Island were actually called *moai*, in Polynesian pop, all Oceanic carvings became members of one happy family: the Tikis. These primitive effigies
were the counteragents in the modern world of plastic and chrome: priapic
monuments to the primal urges that were otherwise suppressed under the or-
dered cleanliness of 50s suburbia.

Although the form they took was inspired by their Polynesian predecessors, American Tikis were more often than not free-form interpretations of several island styles, mixed with a good dose of cartoon whimsy and a dash of modern art. Even those that could be called "authentic" were merely reproductions of the few originals that had survived the "utter abolishment" by zealous missionaries. This liberal attitude towards counterfeiting had actually begun in the Hawaiian Islands with the early Western contacts, seen in the following report from 1825: "The officers of the HBM ship *Blonde*, when here, were anxious to procure some of the ancient idols, to carry home as curios. The demand soon exhausted the stock at hand: to supply the deficiency the Hawaiians made idols, and smoked them, to impart to them an appearance of antiquity, and actually succeeded in the deception." (W .S. W. Ruschenberger, *Extracts from the Journal of an American Naval Officer*, 1841) And over a century later, primitive art collector Pablo Picasso, who was a thrifty flea market shopper, proclaimed: "You don't need the masterpiece to get the idea. The concept or component of a style is entirely accessible in second-rate examples and even fakes." And so American artists, imbued with the spirit of Tiki, did not hesitate to re-create the godheads in their own whimsical manner.

A perfect example of this style is the Tiki that Alec Yuill-Thornton designed for Tiki Bob's bar in San Francisco. Part George Jetson, part modern primitive, this sculpture has very little in common with any Oceanic artifacts. But, together with the signature Tiki of Stephen Crane's Luau, it actually marks the beginning of Tiki style. For the first time, a Tiki was employed as a logo, serving as an entrance guardian, appearing as an icon on the menu and matchbooks, and assuming the form of mugs and salt and pepper shakers.

"Sneaky" Bob Bryant had worked as Trader Vic's bar manager, but when they had a falling out in 1955, Bob moved down a block from the Trader's Cosmo Place location and opened his own bar. An attempt to franchise his concept at the Capitol Inn in Sacramento was short lived. Bob also opened *Tiki Bob's Mainland* on Bush Street where he offered lingerie fashion shows to draw in the business crowd at lunchtime.

Thus Tiki became the star in the Polynesian pop theater, his name christening a multitude of establishments across America from Alabama to Alaska, and his many varied forms adorning just as many "watering holes of the civilization weary." The Tiki image reached the peak of its prominence when it was used as a logo for the Warner Brothers TV series *Hawaiian Eye,* which was beamed into American living rooms from 1959 to 1963, subliminally implanting its archetypal form into the minds of the hypnotized suburbanites.

But just as Tiki fever reached its peak, the big generational divide of the 60s put an end to it. The children of the Tiki revellers decided to create their own Nirvana, where Free Love and otherworldly happiness became an immediate reality. Alcohol was no longer the drug of choice as marihuana and psychedelics became recreational avocations and the sexual revolution seemingly did away with all Puritan notions of monogamy. Together with the tropical cocktails, the greasy sweet faux-Chinese cuisine termed "Polynesian" clashed with the growing health food consciousness.

A NEW WORLD OF

Enchantment

Island drums echo your foot-steps as you enter this Poly-nesian posada yielding unfor-gettable revelry for pleasure seekers and adventurous ap-petites. Here you tread on en-chanted grounds of an authen-tic Polynesian Village recre-ated with captivating mystery and beauty . . . the tempting thrills of the Tahitian Room . . . the haunting delights of the Hawaiian Room . . . the splendors of the Samoan Hut . . . and the carefree relaxa-tion in the Cannibal Cocktail Lounge.

Polynesian Village

Exotic Food and Drink

TIKI BOB

POST AND TAYLOR   SAN FRANCISCO

POLYNESIAN CHOW AND

The "British invasion" shifted the young generation's attention toward another strange foreign cult, the Beatles. The Kinks lamented a plastic Polynesia in "Holiday in Waikiki," whining "… and even all the grass skirts were PVC!"

Just as two centuries earlier the Polynesian natives had realized that the white explorers were not gods when they drew Captain Cook's blood in the skirmish at Kealakekua Bay and were able to kill him, Americans suffered a traumatic blow to their own godliness when President Kennedy was killed in 1963. It was the beginning of the end, marking the loss of youthful innocence in their own eyes and those of the world.

Exotica and the Tiki style were denounced as contrived rituals of the imperialist establishment at the same time that the Vietnam war developed into an ugly mistake, with native huts and palm trees burning on TV. Young protesters were marching on the Capitol in Washington while Richard Nixon was drinking Mai Tai's at his favorite hang out, the Washington *Trader Vic's*.

TIKI LODGE

EXOTIC
Atmosphere
TIKI ISLAND
3743 SO. WESTERN AVE.
LOS ANGELES

TiKi-KAi
371-7588

509 No. Riverside
Medford, Ore. 97501

820
N AVE.
BAR
ove
rks.
KA ·
FOR SAFETY

JOSEPH MASSAGLIA JR., PRES.

the
Tiki-Jo
...featuring
POLYNESIAN FOOD
EXOTIC DRINKS

STRIKE ON BACK COVER

HOST COVER BEFORE STRIK

Tiki Men's Salon
IN THE
TAHITIAN VILLAGE
13519 LAKEWOOD BLVD.
DOWNEY, CALIF.
★ ★ ★
HAIR STYLING

PETE ARMENTA
SE COVER ――― FOR SAFETY

ut
VD.

1718 WALNUT
pub Tiki
PARK
FREE
1815 Walnut

Everything extravagant
but the Prices!

the
pub

341-7766

Club
Tiki

Please Close Cover Before Striking

★ ★ ★
ENTERTAINMENT
Dancing
ROSCOE
at DESOTO
CANOGA PARK
Host - FLORIAN

In the 70s, the thus segregated Polynesian style was watered down further through a certain "Jimmy Buffetization,"—the introduction of a generic tropical island theme with no definite identity. Be it the Caribbean, Mexico, or Polynesia, everywhere was Margharita-ville. The popular TV show *Fantasy Island* typified this new "politically correct" detachment from cultural complicity, creating a world of white wicker colonial-style decor mixed with exotic plants.

The fern bar replaced the Tiki bar.

The 1980s was the decade of destruction—the abolishment of Tiki and his culture. Either completely razed or renovated beyond recognition, Polynesian palaces disappeared without ever having been acknowledged as a unique facet of American pop culture. Purely an expression of a popular fad, they had always been denounced and ignored by the culture critics in their own time; now they represented merely an embarrassing lapse of taste. Unnoticed and without mourning, a whole tradition vanished.

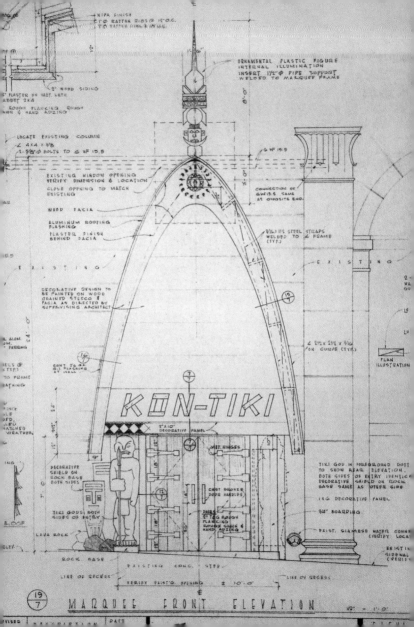

ERECTING A TIKI TEMPLE

The construction of a "Hale Tiki" (House of Tiki) was an elaborate undertaking, not only because of the various exotic materials used, but owing to the unusual concepts that were employed to fill the attending Tiki devotees with amazement and delight as they filled themselves with tropical libations.

This chapter will enlighten the reader on the exterior and interior motifs that define the architecture of Tiki style, and in so doing help establish the thus-far unrecognized style as a part of American pop culture. Though there is a distinct tradition that has been followed since Don the Beachcomber, with certain devices being employed and elaborated on again and again, what characterizes Tiki style is how the individual entrepreneurs who were struck with Tiki fever

 HALE TIKI

NATIVE DWELLINGS
OF THE PACIFIC AREA

re-created it in their own way. From fake interior jungles to drink presentation rituals, personal imaginations ran wild as American developers followed the call of Tiki and conjured up their subjective versions of a South Seas sanctuary.

The preferred architectural concept was that of the A-frame. Was it just a timely coincidence that towards the end of the 1950s the new primitivism of the Tiki style concurred with its antithesis, the futuristic jet age look, or was one born as a necessary reaction to the other? In any case, both were united gloriously in the A-frame. With Eero Saarinen's TWA Terminal and Frank Lloyd Wright's First Unitarian Church, jetting gables became a favorite plaything of modern architects, mirroring the space-age optimism also found in Cadillac tail fins.

It so happened that the majority of traditional Oceanic domiciles were palm huts, and as such A-shaped. But since the native structures of the Polynesians were—with the exception of the elaborately carved Maori meeting houses—rather plain, other South Sea culture groups were enlisted. The New Guinea cult house, or *Haus Tambaran*, with its sweeping gable and mask-decorated front, and the ceremonial meeting house as found on Palau, Micronesia, (also known as the men's club house!) with its colorful story-board paintings, were the inspiration for many American Tiki temples. The Jetsons met the Flintstones as middle-class modern primitives parked their shuttle crafts in front of these spaceships from planet Tiki and willingly entered the dimension barrier to another world where for a while they could become members of the Tiki tribe.

A-frames were easy to build, and so traditional structures like Wisconsin log cabins or classic downtown business buildings were transformed into pagan palaces by the addition of a peaked entrance. Chinese restaurants "updated" their style with the hut look to benefit from the Polynesian craze. But what happened behind the big A?

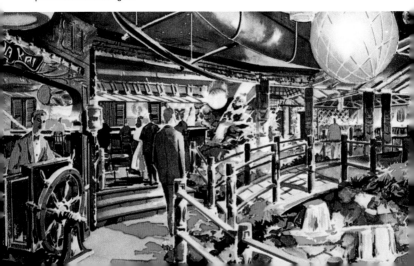

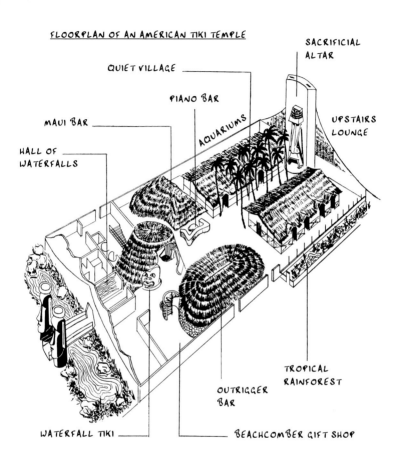

FLOORPLAN OF AN AMERICAN TIKI TEMPLE

SACRIFICIAL ALTAR

QUIET VILLAGE

PIANO BAR

MAUI BAR

AQUARIUMS

UPSTAIRS LOUNGE

HALL OF WATERFALLS

TROPICAL RAINFOREST

WATERFALL TIKI

OUTRIGGER BAR

BEACHCOMBER GIFT SHOP

To symbolize the threshold to another reality, the entrance often required traversing a bridge crossing a stream fed by a lava rock waterfall. The archetypal elements of fire and water were brought into play with gas-fed Tiki torches (sometimes installed as beacons on top of the gables) and exterior and interior waterfalls that provided a subtly gurgling background. Imposing Tikis flanked the entrance, popped out of the jungle foliage, and were used as support posts and other architectural details.

The interior was a multi-layered environment appealing to all the senses. The various rooms with evocative names like "Black Hole of Calcutta" or "Lounge of the Seven Pleasures" were constructed from floor-to-ceiling with exotic woods, bamboo, rattan, Tapa cloth, and other organic naturals. Primitive weapons and masks hung on the walls, while beachcomber lamps and assorted flotsam on the ceiling provided the next layer. Murals of island life and three-dimensional dioramas further enhanced the illusion of being in a faraway place.

TROPICS

The Waikiki Room

The Polynesian Room

The Bamboo Lounge

The Outrigger Bar

The Surfboard Lounge

The Lanai Room

Reservations TAYLOR 6201-2883

4:30 P.M. till 2:30 A.M.

Sundays 12 till 9:30 P.M.

1721 N. Main St.

Dayton's Finest

"Goodie" Sable

Maitre de & Mgr.

Another important texture was that of human skin. Many establishments prided themselves on their scantily clad exotic waitresses; live counterparts to the black velvet paintings that were also part of the regular decor of Tiki lounges. For the white-collar warriors of the 1950s, this exposure held a special allure that was further fueled by the Polynesian floorshows that had become standard entertainment in many South Seas superclubs. That the Samoan Firedancers and Tahitian Hula Girls were often of South American or Asian heritage was not important. The costumes and the music, the exotic textures, the tropical decor, and the potent libations all worked together to dissolve any petty concerns about authenticity, thus allowing the Tiki reveller to become a believer in the hyper-reality of the urban Polynesian paradise.

DON THE BEACHCOMBER– FOUNDING FATHER OF POLYNESIAN POP

Hollywood, 1934: America's "noble experiment" with prohibition had just ended. High-proof alcohol was in demand, and an emigré restauranteur from New Orleans named Ernest Beaumont-Gantt decided to experiment with rum. Maybe inspired by his home town's pirate history or the fact that his father, who owned a hotel in New Orleans, had taken him on trips to Jamaica, Ernest opened a small bar on McCadden Place in Hollywood, propped up some fake palm trees, and named it *Don the Beachcomber*. Here he blended and mixed the liquid gold like an alchemist in search of the sorcerer's stone, creating potent concoctions that allowed his customers temporarily to escape to distant shores, while outside the big city life rushed by.

Ernest identified with the Beachcomber persona so strongly that he legally changed his name to Donn Beach. Soon his expert mixology attracted the alcohol- and atmosphere-hungry film crowd, and in 1937 he expanded his operation into a South Seas hideaway that was to become the blueprint for the many entrepeneurs who would follow in his footsteps: Like an island in the urban sea, the Polynesian paradise that Donn designed was meant to be a refuge from the teaming metropolis that surrounded it.

Upon entering, all the senses were assailed: Exotic materials like bamboo, lahaula matts, and imported woods provided the basic texture. Tropical plants, fresh flower leis, and bunches of bananas and coconuts cultivated the jungle atmosphere, while native weapons and other Oceanic artifacts spoke of savage civilizations. Jetsam and flotsam from the four corners of the world hung from the ceiling, amplifying the illusion of having arrived at some distant port of pleasure. An intermittent man-made rain-on-the-roof effect gave the impression of having escaped from a tropical downpour, while continous soft background music further lulled the patrons into exotic reveries. All this was enhanced by the effect of Don's potent cocktail creations that were sometimes served in whole pineapples, or at least heavily decorated with intriguing garnishes.

But what Donn Beach possessed in showmanship and imagination, he lacked in business smarts. This aspect was taken care of by his wife Cora Irene "Sunny" Sund. She had proposed a business partnership that flowered into a marriage in 1937, only to end in divorce three years later. But she kept a firm grip on the shop—so firm that when Donn returned from his stint as an air force colonel at the end of WW II, he found himself ousted from his own bailiwick. Sunny, who had directed the opening of the first franchise in Chicago in 1940, was now firmly in charge of the operation and did not need Don anymore, except in name.

Cantonese food and
original rum cocktails
presented in an authentic
Polynesian atmosphe

Sunny Sund,
President

HOW DADDY BE
A
BEACHCOMBER

BY MARILYN HENLEY

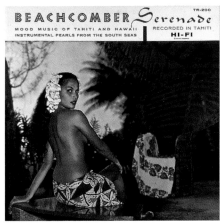

BEACHCOMBER *Serenade* TR-200
MOOD MUSIC OF TAHITI AND HAWAII RECORDED IN TAHITI
INSTRUMENTAL PEARLS FROM THE SOUTH SEAS HI-FI

Always more of an originator than a manager, Donn struck a deal to remain in an advisory position at the mainland *Don the Beachcomber's* while turning his creative energies to his pet project: opening his own place in Hawaii.

But Donn had also created an image, a figure: that of the 20th century urban beachcomber, an individual somewhere between well-travelled connoisseur, beach beatnik, and marina swinger. In the history of Polynesian pop other Beachnik characters appeared, most notable among them Ely Hedley, also known as "the original Beachcomber." A luckless grocer from Oklahoma, he had followed the call of the Pacific Ocean and moved his family to Whites Point, a beach cove near San Pedro in Los Angeles. Here he, his wife, and four daughters built their house out of actual driftwood and started a successful business making lamps and furniture with the flotsam that washed onto their front yard. Ely became so well known for his "Beachcomber Moderne" style that he was hired to decorate Tiki temples like *Trader Dick's* and *Harvey's* in Nevada. When the Tiki fever hit, he started carving Tikis and opened his *Island Trade Store*, first in Huntington Beach, later in Adventureland in Disneyland. After making his definite mark on Tiki style, Ely Hedley retired to the Islander apartments in Santa Ana that he himself had decorated.

In the interim, *Don the Beachcomber* had become a commercial logo, the business changing hands twice and ending up under the ownership of the Getty Corporation. The figure had been modernized from Don's actual likeness

ARE FUN...

CKTAIL MIXES

SCORPION

MIAMI BEACH'S FINEST

Beachcomber

RESORT MOTEL

189th ST.
ON THE OCEAN

MIAMI BEACH
FLORIDA

NE 6-6600

the
BEACHCOMBER
OSWEGO, OREGON
"On the Lake"

BEACHCOMBER
DON'S
CORK 'N' BOTTLE

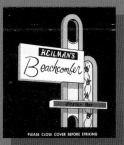

HEILMAN'S
Beachcomber

Jester Bar

PLEASE CLOSE COVER BEFORE STRIKING

67

into an anonymous suave swinger. The franchise had grown to 16 locations—some, like the Dallas and the Marina Del Rey facilities, looking like brown UFOs. Other Polynesiacs all over the States felt inspired by the Beachcomber concept, but none achieved Don's flair. He, meanwhile, had built himself a new kingdom at his International Market place in Waikiki. Here he continued to innovate and create "new ways of doing things" for Polynesia Americana. After Donn passed away in 1987, the remnants of the chain that bore his name closed within a few years, having in any case been devoid of his mana for a long time. But his formative influence on the phenomenon of Polynesian pop is unforgotten.

Leeteg Original from the Collection of Don the Beachcomber

DON THE
BEACHCOMBER®

TRADER VIC –
THE AMBASSADOR OF GOOD TASTE

The Americanization of Tiki as the god of recreation was a gradual process. One of his greatest emissaries was a man named Victor Bergeron, better known as Trader Vic. It was not so much that he openly glorified the godhead per se—he even utilized his own mythological figures, the *Menehune*, or "little people" of Polynesian legends—but beginning in the 50s, the Tiki was always by his side, and the Trader was a larger than life figure, an original, one of a dying breed of unique characters lacking in today's public arena.

A patriarch, a gentleman, and a chauvinist in one, Trader Vic was a successful restaurateur and an epicure who encouraged a generation of "sophisticated savages" to "go native" and create their own Polynesias in lounges, backyards, and bowling alleys. He elevated South Seas "chow and grog," as he liked to call it in his gruff manner, to an art. More than Don the Beachcomber, who supposedly found the name for his appetizer creation "Rumaki" by pointing his finger into the flipping pages of a Cook Islands dictionary, Trader Vic was a culinary innovator. After his success with "nouveau Polynesian" fare he was among the first to bring Mexican food to the American public (with his Señor Pico restaurants), and far ahead of his time he lauded sushi as a delicacy to be savored.

It all began at a joint called *Hinky Dinks* in Oakland, across the bay from San Francisco. This was the first establishment Vic built for himself in 1934, a wooden shack erected with his last five hundred bucks. In the history of Polynesian pop there have been certain "power places," like the *Beachcomber* in Hollywood, the *Luau* in Beverly Hills, the Lanai in San Mateo, or the *Bali Hai* in San Diego, that emanated the mana of Tiki. *Hinky Dinks*, soon to become *Trader Vic's*, was one of them. The late Herb Caen, eminent San Francisco columnist, remembered it as "little more than a beer joint, and yet you knew right away it was someplace special. Good places, as opposed to stinkers, have a distinctive and mysterious atmosphere—an immediate feeling of quality, dedication, success and self-confidence." And Victor Bergeron was an ambitious man with a knack for fancy cocktails, and that was exactly what people had a hankering for after the repeal of Prohibition. He went on a research trip to Cuba and Louisiana and studied with the top mixologists on location. But it was his visit to Los Angeles that was most influential. In his biography he reveals:

"We went to a place called the *South Seas* that doesn't exist anymore and even visited *Don the Beachcomber* in Hollywood. In fact, I even bought some stuff from *Don the Beachcomber*. When then I got back to Oakland and told my wife about what I had seen, we agreed to change the name of our restaurant and change the decor. We decided that *Hinky Dinks* was a junky name and that the place should be named after someone we

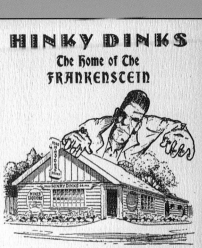

HINKY DINKS
The Home of The
FRANKENSTEIN

Where those merry souls who make drinking a pleasure—
Who achieve contentedness long before capacity,
And who, whenever they drink, prove able to carry it,
enjoy it, and remain gentlemen.

65th Street and San Pablo Avenue   Oakland, California

PRESS OF THE COURIER

could tell a story about. My wife suggested *Trader Vic's* because I was always making a trade with someone. Fine, I became Trader Vic." Consequently, the wooden leg that he had inherited from a bout with tuberculosis as a child (and had entertained his customers with by unexpectedly sticking an icepick into it) became the result of an encounter with a shark, one of the many tales that were in keeping with Vic's new persona.

The candid revelation about the birth of Trader Vic came from a man who had not only equalled but superceded the achievements of his peer and predecessor. Gentleman Vic never had to deny his sources, because he never lost control of his venture as Donn did, and when the Polynesian trend took off in

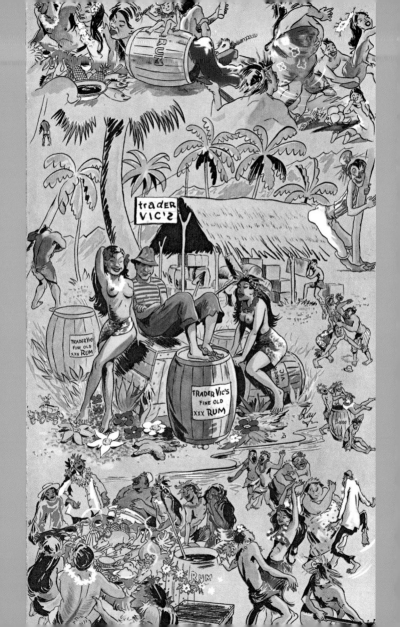

the traders

the 1950s, he was positioned to take full advantage of it. Opening his first outpost, which he called *The Outrigger*, in Seattle in 1949, he followed with a flow of satellite supper clubs throughout the next decades: in San Francisco proper in 1951, Denver in 1954, Beverly Hills in 1955, Chicago in 1957, New York and Havana in 1958, and Portland in 1959. They were followed by places in Boston, Houston, Dallas, Detroit, Atlanta, Kansas City, St. Louis, St. Petersburg, Washington, Vancouver, Scottsdale, London, Munich, and a host of other foreign locations.

Vic further expanded his influence with a string of cocktail and recipe books in which he preferably used merchandise from his new Trader Vic's Food Products company. In these publications he expounded his

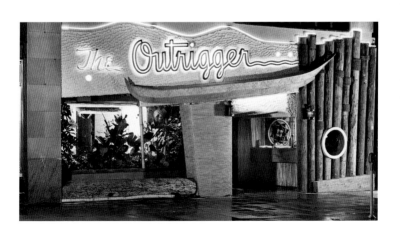

TRADER VIC'S
FOOD AND
GIFT LIST

A SELECTION OF UNUSUAL GIFTS AND EXOTIC FOODS
FROM TRADER VIC'S FOOD PRODUCTS, INC.
9809 SAN PABLO AVE. · BERKELEY 2, CALIF.

Trader Vic's

**TIPS ON
FOOD AND
DRINK**

*Bartender's
Guide* · BY
Trader Vic
ILLUSTRATED BY RAY SULLIVAN

A MANUAL INCLUDING OVER 1500 RECIPES FOR
THE HOME AND PROFESSIONAL BARTENDER

Trader Vic's
THOUGHTS ON BARBECUING

VOODOO GROG

Old
debbil Rum
conjures
throbbing drumbeats
and black magic

ACROSS FROM DICK GRAVES' NUGGET

Trader Dick's
SPARKS, NEVADA

FEATURING BARBEQUED RIBS AND CHICKEN FROM OUR AUTHENTIC ISLAND SMOKE OVEN.

SPARKS, NEVADA - 3 MILES EAST OF RENO

views upon social gatherings and middle-class eating habits in his characteristic Trader Vic lingo, which was quite different from the flowery prose he used in his menus: "I've a lot of pet peeves to get off my chest concerning what cooks when you go over to somebody's house to chisel some food and drinks and I further contend that the average American hostess needs a swift kick in her culinary pants, so let's get about it. The tidbits usually served at cocktail parties simply slay me. After looking at hundreds of silver platters and their contents for many years, I've reached the conclusion that someone must have offered an annual Pulitzer prize for the most deadly hors d'œuvre." The Trader was a salty son of a bitch, and people loved him that way.

When Hawaii became America's vacation destination of choice, Vic was approached to act as food consultant for United Airlines and the hotels of the Matson steamship line, which were the two main tourist transporters between the Islands and America. Earlier, around 1940, he had formed a partnership to open a place in Honolulu but pulled out as the result of a disagreement, leaving the other party the right to use the name in the Islands. The fact that a *Trader Vic's* was opened in Hawaii having originated in California—the same way *Don the Beachcomber*, Stephen Crane's *Kon-Tiki* and *Christian's Hut* proceeded—is curious and supports the claim that Polynesian pop is truly a facet of American pop culture which actually was imported to Hawaii to fulfill the expectations of the tourists.

This growth of the Trader's empire was made possible by the financial resources of major hotel chains like Western (now Westin) and Conny Hilton's. They could afford the elaborate construction a classy Tiki lounge required. And *Trader Vic's* was all class. Other South Sea joints, among them many that copied his monicker, served the foot soldier, whereas Vic's was the officer's club—not because Vic was a snob, but because he wanted to make a buck, and he succeeded in attracting the well-off. But ultimately, this selective clientele was also part of the reason for the chain's demise, because as the upper-class clique that frequented these ports of the palate died out, the younger generations sought out more affordable and less affected surroundings.

Sadly the outposts in Seattle, Washington, Vancouver, Portland, and even San Francisco have closed—some as recently as the 90s—and, in those that are left, misguided renovation efforts during the 1980s caused the characteristic birdcage lamps and other traditional decor to be thrown out as "dust catchers." But hotel hideways like the Chicago and Munich *Trader Vic's* remain (as of this writing) as rare examples of Tiki style.

LUAU

BEVERLY HILLS

STEPHEN CRANE— THE MAN WHO LOVED WOMEN

In Polynesian lore from Mangareva and the Marquesas, Tiki, the first man, is depicted as a trickster and charmer. After all, it was he who created the first woman from mud, immediately proceeding to make all the children of this world with her. So it seems appropriate that the next inheritor of the Tiki torch was a man whose main talents seemed to be socializing and womanizing. An unsuccessful B-movie actor (*Cry of the Werewolf*), his sole claim to fame was that he had been married to Lana Turner. It was a Las Vegas wedding, performed by the same judge who earlier had married Lana to jazz gigolo Artie Shaw. The marriage lasted only five months, but the couple had a daughter, Cheryl, who much later, as a teenager, rose to fame by stabbing Lana's Mafiosi lover, Johnny Stompanato, to death (apparently because she had earlier been molested by another of her mother's suitors, movie Tarzan Lex Barker). But Stephen remained on friendly terms with Lana while he went on seducing other film stars. The owner of Ciro's, Hollywood's main movie hangout in the forties, remarked after seeing Steve show up on three consecutive nights with Ava Gardner, Rita Hayworth, and Lana Turner: "This town's three top queens! I never saw anybody do that."

Luckily Stephen Crane's energies were soon directed towards his other talents: socializing and entertaining. In 1953 he opened his restaurant *The Luau* at 421 Rodeo Drive in Beverly Hills. The site had earlier housed the South Seas joint *The Tropics*, and Stephen elaborated on the theme, while aiming to retain the movie colony clientele. He did this in his own way, as his daughter Cheryl recalls in her biography *Detour- A Hollywood Story:* "He figured since men liked to hang out in spots that attracted women, he needed to bait the place like a honey trap ... At the core of Dad's honey trap was a little-known and never-voiced policy of allowing select and very expensive hookers to mingle discreetly at the bar. Often failed starlets, they were refined and beautifully dressed, their presence drawing men while not offending escorted women customers, who rarely recognized them for what they were."

And to put the effect of the "Beauty and the Beast" archetype to full use, Crane profusely populated his paradise with Tikis, introducing them in his menu: "Of great interest are the TIKIS, the large and delightfully unlovely carvings about you. A TIKI is a pagan god, an idol. While today a majority of our South Seas neighbors are of

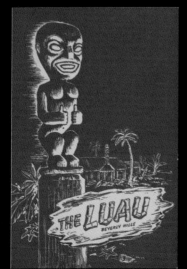

THE LUAU
BEVERLY HILLS

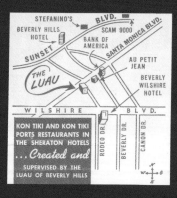

Christian faith, respect and deference is still extended to the gods of the elders, and we have with us here at THE LUAU such TIKIS as the god of rain, the god of sun, the god of war and others. The especially large-mouthed TIKI is the god of drink, The Loud-Mouthed One. The TIKI with the most ample tummy is our favorite, perhaps because he is the god of good food." This whimsical and naive attitude towards another people's extinct religion henceforth characterized Tiki style. For the first time, a Tiki resembling the two entrance-post carvings was used as an emblem on menus, matchbooks, postcards, and as the form for a ceramic lamp base, as well as salt and pepper shakers.

In the rest of the decor, Stephen was drawing strongly on the Beachcomber and Trader traditions—so strongly that art director Florian Gabriel recalls that as a requirement for his job as designer for Stephen Crane and Associates, he was asked to go to *Trader Vic's* at the Beverly Hilton (which once boasted five fifteen-foot-high exterior Tikis) and sketch a corner of the restaurant. He did so successfully, and then and there formed a design team together with George Nakashima, who had previously worked for Welton Becket, architect of the Beverly Hilton. They went on to help construct the satellite islands that SCA began to install in other American cities at the end of the 50s.

The Sheraton Corporation, eager to pull even with Hilton, had invited Crane to re-create his *Luau* in their hotel in Montreal, where it opened as the *Kon Tiki* in 1958, presenting to the astounded public "woodpanels handcarved by the Maoris with special designs to ward off evil spirits, New Guinea spears with bat-wing tips dipped in poison by headhunters, and a sacrificial altar." In the next years establishments in Portland (with three waterfalls!), Chicago, Dallas, Cleveland, and Honolulu followed. The Chicago *Kon-Tiki Ports* and the Dallas *Ports o' Call* elaborated on the armchair traveller concept by giving every dining room a different theme: Papeete, Singapore, Macao, or Saigon. Their stories were pure Polynesian pop poetry: "PAPEETE-One of four exotic moorings at Ports o' Call Restaurant in the penthouse at Southland Center, Dallas, Texas. Nature has been tamed for this tropic hideaway. A waterfall babbles for your pleasure while local wildlife stands motionless to keep you at your ease. But spears and pelts remind the diner that simple life does have its excitements."

Yet the rift that really was soon to create between the Tiki generation and its Vietnam-War-protesting children is probably best examplified by the description of the SAIGON room: "Oriental splendor and opulence mark this Port of Pleasure. Its fortunate inhabitants are surrounded by pure gold leaf, rare silks, fine crystal and once-forbidden temple carvings." What was poetic license in 1960 had turned painfully ironic by 1968. At the end of the seventies, an Iranian consortium offered Stephen Crane 4.1 million dollars for the *Luau*. In 1979 it was razed down right to the sub-basement, a signal for end of the Tiki era.

MACAO

AIGON

ORE

PAPEETE

CREATED AND SUPERVISED BY

Kon-Tiki

Steve Crane

FOR THE

SHERATON-MT. ROYAL

1455 PEEL STREET, MONTREAL, CANADA

Ports of Pleasure

LES BAXTER

DANNY BALSZ–
THE PRODIGAL SON

The figure of Danny Balsz does not fall seamlessly into the succession of Polynesian pop's elders. He neither started a chain, nor did he come up with culinary or alcoholic innovations. He did not concern himself with quality as much as with quantity. For Danny Balsz, bigger was better, so he built the biggest volcano on the largest Polynesian luau grounds in the land. Here every night a Tiki maiden was thrown into its fiery cavity as sacrifice, while Tahitian dancers in costumes that borrowed more from Las Vegas than from the South Sea islands swayed to the rhythms of various bands. When he found out that the Hawaiians supposedly believed that the more Tikis you had in your house the more luck you had, he surrounded himself with wooden effigies of all shapes and sizes and called the place THE TIKIS. More gods, more dancers, more food and drink for more than 3000 customers a night—it was Tiki for the masses, and Danny was Mr. Tiki!

THE TIKIS represents the culmination of the Tiki era, which peaked with unprecedented grandeur and decadence before crumbling into cultural oblivion. Stumbling upon the ruins of this forgotten Disneyland of the gods, I knew that its story had to be told one day. Before me lay the lost planet of the Tikis, the elephant graveyard of an extinct species. What had led to the demise of this once grand civilization? The son of a nightclub owner in the bordertown of Mexicali, Danny Balsz moved to East L. A. with memories of forbidden glamor. He worked for ten years as a slaughter house butcher, until he decided to go into landscaping, specializing in waterfalls. In 1958 Danny was getting some supplies at a Japanese nursery in Monterey

Park, a rural Los Angeles suburb wedged between four freeways. Stopping at a neighboring egg ranch, he met the owner, Doris Samson. Four months later they were married. While helping Doris with her hens, Danny was developing his landscaping skills, slowly transforming the quarter-acre property into a tropical garden. In 1960 two college students asked Danny if they could hold a luau party on the lot. At this time, luau grounds for party rentals were springing up everywhere in the southland. Danny and Doris decided to slaughter all their chickens and go into the Polynesian party business. The timing was right, the place took off, and year for year Danny was pouring and sculpting more and more concrete into lava tunnels, stalagtite caves, and waterfalls, single handedly creating his own Xanadu.

By the late 60s, his predominantly blue-collar clientele was arriving by the busload from aircraft plants and trucking companies. The necessary supplies, such as 50,000 leis from the plastic-lei factory in Hughestown, Pennsylvania, and tons of pineapples, were paid for in cash, and if there was money left, Danny bought more Tikis. "I had everything, man: Money, cars, rings!" reminisced Danny. But he wanted more. Danny's luck ran out when he committed the eternal sin: His fall from grace was was occasioned by his falling in love with Leilani, a Mormon Hawaiian dancer at *THE TIKIS*. The union of the *haole* and *wahine* was not sanctified by the gods, and

even less so by Danny's wife and children, who had been the backbone of his family operation. And under pressure from fed-up neighbors, the city council revoked his entertainment license. The Polynesian three-ring circus was over, it seemed. But Danny Balsz was a driven man. He packed up his Tikis and built them a new home at Lake Elsinore, further south of L. A. There he labored for years, re-erecting a complete new lava-land. Patiently his Tikis stood guard over it, awaiting the grand re-opening. But the times had changed, and the great day never came.

"The light that burns twice as bright burns half as long, and you have burned so very, very brightly. You're the prodigal son!"

"But I've done questionable things …"

"Also extraordinary things, revelled in your time …"

(from Ridley Scott's *Bladerunner*)

KON-TIKI, AKU AKU, AND THOR

"The unsolved mysteries of the South Seas had fascinated me. There must be a rational solution to them, and I had made my objective the identification of the legendary hero TIKI."

Thus spoke a young Norwegian zoologist named Thor Heyerdahl in 1937, while struggling to survive on his island hideway of Fatu Hiva in the Marquesas, where he and his wife were sharing a pre-hippy existence. Thor and Liv had decided to forsake civilization and go "back to nature," living like primitives while researching the local fauna for his Oslo university. But when Thor heard old Tei Tetua, the last native who had tasted "Long Pig" (man), recite an old folk tale by the evening fire, everything changed. "Tiki, he was both god and chief. It was Tiki who brought my ancestors to these islands on which we live. Before that we lived in a great land far beyond the sea."

Thor was inspired to shift his object of study from snails and giant poisonous centipedes to the origin of the Polynesian race. He had noticed the likeness of the Marquesan stone tikis and petroglyphs to Incan idols in Peru, and for the next ten years he worked on his theory that the Pre-Incan high priest and sun-king Kon-Tici Viracocha, who had been forced to flee Peru by a waring chieftain, was identical with the Polynesian ancestor god, Tiki. Encountering nothing but scournful resistance from archeologists, ethnologists, linguists, and sociol-

THE AMAZING ADVENTURE OF SIX MEN ON A RAFT ACROSS THE PACIFIC! TRUE! THRILLING!

SOL LESSER

presents

KON-T

Photographed by the men who lived it... Told by **THOR HEYERDAH**

Produced by OLLE NORDEMAR · Music by SUNE WALDIMIR · An Art

HOW 'KON-TIKI' GOT ITS NAME

Tiki was the name of the first great chief on Tahiti. He was regarded by the inhabitants as their divine ancestor, and stone statues like this were erected to his honor on many Polynesian islands.

KI

...or of the best-selling book.

...buted by RKO RADIO PICTURES

51 \ 122

KON TIKI RESTAURANT & MOTO[R]

RIVERSIDE · CALIFORNIA

ARMET & DAVIS A.I.A. ARCHITECTS

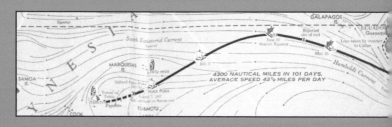

ogists, Thor set out to prove his theory in practice. He built a pre-Columbian balsa log raft, without using a single spike, nail, or wire rope, named it "Kon-Tiki," and proceeded to let himself and his five Scandinavian crewmen drift on the Humboldt Current from Peru to Polynesia.

After only three months on the open sea, the Kon-Tiki succeeded in reaching the Polynesian shores. The book about the voyage entitled The Kon-Tiki Expedition was first published in Norway in 1948, where it received unfavorable reviews, the whole endeavor being likened to "going over the Niagara Falls in a barrel." But this criticism did not deter the public's interest in the intrepid undertaking.

Shortly after publication in England and America in 1950, it became evident that the publishers had a bestseller on their hands. Eventually Kon -Tiki was translated into sixty different languages—the only book other than the Bible to reach this wide distribution. The film shot on the voyage met a similar fate, first being rejected by American distributors because of its technical flaws. Nevertheless it received the 1951 Academy Award for best documentary and was seen by millions of people. The world had just come out of the trauma of the Second World War and was longing for pacifist adventure.

The unprecedented worldwide Kon-Tiki fever further fueled America's fascination with Polynesian culture. Though "Tiki style" as a term was not in use during the 50s and 60s, the vernacular "Kon-Tiki style" was a popular way to refer to Polynesian architecture. Thor and Tiki, the Norse god of thunder and the Polynesian god of the sun, had united to become popular heroes. Heyerdahl's 1955 book about his Easter Island expedition, Aku Aku, proved equally influential on Polynesian pop. The book's cover became such a popular icon that the giant stone statues, correctly termed moai, became known as Aku Aku heads, or even Aku-Tikis, making them into a widespread theme in American Tikidom.

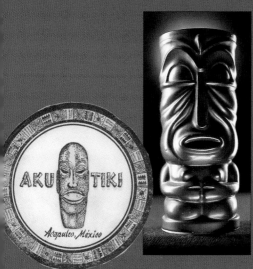

AKU TIKI
Acapulco, México

AKU TIKI
LOUNGE
LINCOLN, NEBR. "

PEGGY LEE

MARGARET WHITING

GORDON MacRAE

songs from
RODGERS & HAMMERSTEIN'S
"SOUTH PACIFIC"

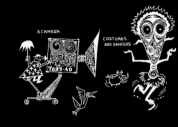

13

JAMES MICHENER AND BALI HAI

"Bali Hai may call you, any night, any day.
In your heart you hear it call you, come away,
come away.
Bali Hai will whisper, on the wind, on the sea,
here am I, your special island, come to me,
come to me.
Your own special hopes, your own special
dreams, loom on the hillside and shine in the
stream.
If you try, you will find me, where the sky
meets the sea,
here am I, your special island, come to me,
come to me."

(Rodgers & Hammerstein's South Pacific)

Thor was not the only bestselling author to make his mark on Polynesian pop. During the Second World War a whole generation of American servicemen had come into direct contact with Pacific island culture. James Michener had been among them, and his fictional account of their plight, Tales of the South Pacific, won him the 1948 Pulitzer Prize and tremendous popular success. A Broadway musical and a Cinemascope movie romanticized the actual hardships of war so successfully that a new idiom for the "exotic paradise" was created: the fictional "Bali Ha'i," the isle of the women. It became the new Shangri-La, everyman's dream island.

It was here that the novel's hero, Lt. Cable, experienced the age-old male fantasy of unconstrained love with a young exotic beauty. The story's protagonist is allowed the privilege of visiting the island, "a jewel of the vast ocean," on which "the French, with Gallic foresight and knowledge in these things, had housed all young women from the islands. Every girl, no matter how ugly or what her color, who might normally be raped by Americans was hidden on Bali Ha'i." (Michener)

As lieutnant Cable's boat anchors, he is envied by every 1950s male reader: "For the first time in his life he had seen so many women, in fact any women, walking about with no clothes on above their hips …[L]ike the jungle, like the fruits of the jungle, adolescent girls seemed to abound in unbelievable profusion." (Michener)

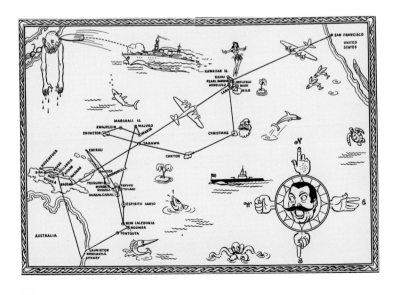

Cable is swiftly rescued from the swarming maidens by the native matron Bloody Mary who wastes no time in setting him up with her beautiful virgin daughter, Liat. In the film our hero enters a romantic palm hut where Liat, a stunning beauty, awaits him, ready for love. No words are spoken—longing eyes, trembling lips: love is immediate and deep. The South Sea archetypes must be true, after all.

The fact that Americans from all walks of life had suddenly been exposed first hand to a completely strange culture left an indelible impression on America itself: "What am I doing here? How did I, Joe Cable of Philadelphia, wind up out here? This is Bali Ha'i, and a year ago I never heard of it. What am I doing here?" (Michener) The attitude was one of

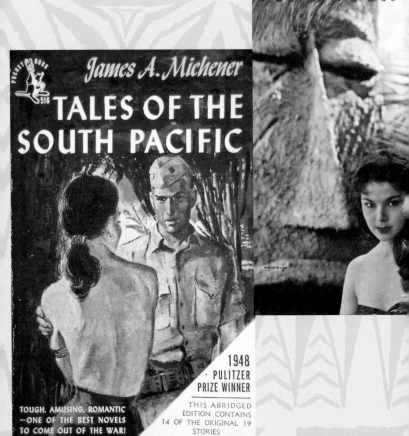

AND

LIBERTY

exotic sounds of
MARTIN DENNY

A999

Every Book Complete

A BANTAM GIANT 35¢

JAMES A. MICHENER

Author of "Tales OF THE South Pacific"

Return to Paradise

WATCHING NAVEL MANEUVERS!

POLYNESIAN PARADISE

AUTHENTIC CANTONESE
CUISINE
•
EXOTIC
POLYNESIAN DRINKS

RESERVATIONS ADVISED

PHONE FA. 9859

BALI HA'I
at the beach

NEW ORLEANS, LA.

boyish wonder, and because the soldiers had been received warmly as saviors from the despised Japanese, the memories that remained of the South Pacific service were mostly of an exciting or pleasant nature. Consequently all over the U. S.A., little Bali Hai's popped up, serving those who had been there as well as those who had not.

James Michener followed the success of South Pacific with Return to Paradise in 1951. His further works included Rascals in Paradise (1957, with an account of Edgar Leeteg's life) and Hawaii (1959), establishing him firmly as the most-read author on Polynesia in the 50s.

The actual Bali Ha'i had been visited by Michener on the islet of Mono, near Guadalcanal. He remembered it as "a filthy, unpleasant village," but made a note of its name because he liked "its musical quality." This did not keep the Polynesian pop myth of Bali Ha'i from eventually getting re-imported to French Polynesia. In 1961, obviously infected by Tiki fever, a lawyer, a stockbroker, and a sporting goods salesman decided to abandon their civilized lives in the Los Angeles suburb of Newport Beach and made the move to Tahiti. Here they opened a hotel—and named it Bali Hai, of course. Fiction had conquered fact, as so often in Polynesian pop.

Polynesian Floor Shows

South Pacific Room

THURSDAY
10:15 p.m.

SUNDAY
10:15 p.m.

FRIDAY
10:00 p.m.
and
12:00 p.m.

SATURDAY
10:00 p.m.
and
12:00 p.m.

SHELTER ISLAND'S BALI HAI RESTAURANT POINT LOMA, CALIF.

HOTEL
BaLi
Hai

FRENCH POLYNESIA

MOOREA

RAIATEA

119

Lapu Lapu

Exotic tropical fruit nectars harmoniously blended with the finest of imported rums.

Gold Cup

A frosty medley of fine Jamaican Rums, tree-ripened limes and golden nectar of the tropical sun.

Scorpion

A South Seas concoction of rums, fruit juices and brandy with a whisper of almond bedecked with gardenias and served with long straws.

Islander

MIXOLOGISTS & CONCOCTIONS

BY JEFF BERRY

What kind of restaurant could get away with calling canned fruit on a scoop of cottage cheese "Ports Of Desire"? The *Luau* could—largely because they served the best exotic rum drinks in Beverly Hills. Such drinks were the fuel that kept the wheels of commerce turning for Polynesian restauranteurs. More than mere cocktails, from the beginning they were presented as Technicolor fantasies that meant as much for the eye as for the tongue and served with elaborate garnishes in even more elaborate vessels. Even the ice that kept them cold was sculpted into fanciful shapes, molded into a cone frozen around your straw, or into an igloo so that your drink arrived "sleeping in a cove of ice." A drink was just as likely to arrive smoking, flaming, or bedecked with a floating gardenia in which a hidden pearl awaited your discovery.

This was the cocktail as Conversation Piece. When you left a Polynesian restaurant, you didn't talk about the food—you talked about the "Mystery Drink," or the "Penang Afrididi," or "Pele's Bucket Of Fire." And the management itself usually started the conversation going on the menu, where flowery, poetic descriptions accompanied fetishistically rendered color illustrations of a drink. Said *The Islander* of its

Mount Kilauea, "An eruption of the finest in imported rums fired with the sacred nectars of the Tiki Gods."

As you might expect, these concoctions didn't always taste as good as they looked. But the best tropical drinks could be complex, layered, at once subtle and voluptuous, with a delicate balance between sweet and sour, strong and light, fruity and dry. And the best tropical drinks originated at *Don The Beachcomber's*.

When Don opened his first bar in 1934, rum was déclassé. Alcoholics were "rummies." Only sailors and stewbums drank demon rum; the smart set drank whiskey and gin. So why didn't Don invent whiskey and gin drinks? Because rum was cheaper. When Prohibition ended, cases of the stuff could be had for as little as 70 cents a quart. In Don's case, frugality was the mother of invention. But Don didn't create his "Rum Rhapsodies" out of thin air. Nash Aranas, former supervisor and "director of authenticity" for the Beachcomber restaurant chain, acknowledged in 1989 that Don had "spent time in the West Indies where he got the rum idea."

"Don would sit there all day with his cronies mixing drinks," remembers Aranas. "He would test, test, test, test, like a mad scientist." The combinations were endless and endlessly varied, resulting in such popular early inventions as the Vicious Virgin, the Shark's Tooth, the Cobra's Fang, the Dr. Funk, and the Missionary's Downfall. Legend has it that Don's most famous drink, the Zombie, was improvised on the spot to help a hungover customer get through an important business meeting. When asked later how the

ZOMBIE

Created at Don the Beachcomber, Hollywood in 1934. Often imitated, but never duplicated.

PI YI

Crushed fresh Hawaiian fruits and light Cuban Rums served in a hollowed-out baby pineapple.

TAHITIAN RUM PUNCH

Exotic tropical fruits admirably blended with Mexican limes and old Cuban Rums.

cure worked, the customer said, "I felt like the living dead—it made a Zombie out of me." But the copy from a 1941 *Beachcomber* menu offers a different origin myth: "The Zombie didn't just happen. It is the result of a long and expensive process of evolution. In the experiments leading up to the Zombie, three-and-a-half cases of assorted rums were used and found their way down the drain so that you may now enjoy this potent 'mender of broken dreams'."

In a conversation shortly before his death, veteran mixologist Ray Buhen, one of the original *Beachcomber* employees in '34, told yet another story. "Don was a nice guy," recalled Buhen, who went on to open his own bar, the *Tiki Ti,* 27 years later. "But he'd say anything. He said he invented the Zombie, but he didn't. Or hardly any of his drinks." Buhen maintained that most of this work was done by "The Four Boys," a quartet of Filipino assistants Don had working behind the bar—a heretical notion, to be sure, but Ray's

MYSTERY BLOSSOM 2.75
A flowering creation for the sensuous at

KAHIKI COFFEE GROG 2.00
Awaken the slow the dawn

PINA PASSION 3.50
Heightens the desire!

IDOL'S CAST 3.25
A fine blend of rums
with brandy

JUNGLE FEVER
Throbbing drums and black mag

PORT LIGHT 2.80
Bourbon lovers take this
left turn

WIDOW'S WAIL 2.40
This potent gin drink   quieteth the widow.

KAHIKI PEARL 2.00
This treasure just couldn't stay hidden for long

NATIVE NECTAR 2.80
Nectar of the Tiki Gods laced with blessed rums.

BAHIA 2.85
Light and white rums—listen to the   drums!

NAVY GROG 3.50
21 guns! The world renowned
standard and justly so.

SATAN'S SIN 2.65
Once in a lifetime!

POLYNESIAN SPELL 1.80
Gin laced with brandy will put you "under"

MAIDEN'S PRAYER 1.90
Barbados rum may be her answer

Brought t
Kahiki My

TONGA TALE 2.30
Captain Coury had a story
worth repeating.

Rum — the magic ing
glowing sunsets in the rolling
romance, the pulsating rhythm

This is the love-child of the ancient
adventurous captains like Magellan ar
effects of the many dark, light and ve
of the Mango Papaya, Guava, Cocon
of Polynesia.

These exciting drinks have been
Only in that way can one fu
to practice the art of

MAI-TAI 3.25
Mai-Tai means "the best"   with 15-year-old
Special Reserve   Jamaican Rum.

PAGO PASSAGE
Full sails topped with champagne.

POLYNESIAN ENTERPRISES, INC 1963

Ki Drink Menu

SMOKING ERUPTION
Where there's smoke,
there's fire! 3.50

ZOMBIE
Built lethal... a mighty combination
laced with Damerara 151. 3.60

FOG CUTTER
Why be confused, light the way
with this slicer 3.00

KAHIKI SWIZZLE
A whirlpool of rums subtly blended 3.00

STARBOARD LIGHT
The right course for Scotch drinkers. 2.90

HEADHUNTER
Take care you don't lose
your head! 3.25

MISTY ISLE
Light and medium rum,
blended with a liqueur
may fog you up 2.75

ASTARD
oubles into little ones. 3.30

POTENT POTION
Refreshing mixture of vodka sherry wine
and tropical juices 2.80

HOT BUTTERED RUM
The traditional 'warmer' of hearts
and friendships 2.00

DERBY DAIQUIRI
A qualified winner every time. 1.90

COCONUT KISS
Gin and Coco Lopez in a coconut shell
A real soother! 3.00

PENANG #1
This blend of rare rum and brandy calls for #2. 2.90

NK

ur or more 10.00

e to the land of the brilliantly
mysterious key to enchantment and
of a civilization now fast ebbing away
fine that slowed and delayed the journeys of
tout hearted seamen set about to research the
d via the West Indies blended with the juices
uit and the myriad of almost unknown fruits

Kahiki. Savor them slowly. Enjoy them,
antically apart – and yet enable one

BLUE HURRICANE
Batten down the hatches!

BACKSCRATCHER
Rum, vodka, and brandy for that itch you can't scratch. 3.50

INSTANT URGE
Don't let the cool green
fool you. 1.85

MALAYAN MIST
A delicious pink fog of rum
and vodka 2.50

credentials as a source are impeccable: 62 years as a mixologist in the most famous Polynesian palaooo, from the *Seven Seas* and the *Luau* to the *China Trader* and his own bar, serving the likes of Clark Gable, Charlie Chaplin, Buster Keaton, the Marx Brothers, and Marlon Brando.

Whatever their origins, Don's drinks became so popular so quickly that "four boys" soon were not enough. Don eventually had to hire seven full-time bartenders, each specializing in different drinks. Behind them were still more Filipino assistants, coring pineapples with piano wire, shaving big blocks of ice until their arms ached, and squeezing limes until the citric acid ate into their fingernails. To add insult to injury, strict security was enforced to make sure none of these assistants could memorize Don's secret recipes. Instead of labels, the bottles were identified only by numbers and letters. According to a 1948 Saturday Evening Post article, "The recipes are in code and the mixers follow a pattern of code symbols indicating premixed ingredients, rather than actual names of fruit concentrates and rum brands. In this way, even if a rival restauranteur makes a raid on the Beachcomber help ... the renegade cannot take Don's recipes with him."

If Don was the Great White Father of the tropical drink, he had many Prodigal Sons. Rip-offs occured almost as soon as Don opened. But while others were content to imitate Don, Trader Vic was more ambitious. "I didn't know a damn thing about that kind of booze," he wrote in his autobiography, "and I thought I'd like to learn." He traveled far and wide, observing internationally renowned mixologists such as Havana's Constantine Ribailagua (who created the *Papa Dobles* grapefruit daiquiri for Ernest Hemingway) and New Orleans' Albert Martin (of Ramos Fizz fame). By the time he returned to his Oakland saloon, Trader Vic was no longer an imitator. He was an innovator. When Vic gave birth to the Scorpion, the Samoan Fog Cutter, and the Mai Tai, all of a sudden *he* became the one everybody was ripping off. "This aggravates my ulcer completely," he fumed when bars from Tahiti to Tulsa began taking credit for the Mai Tai. "Anyone who says I didn't create this drink," maintained Vic, "is a dirty stinker." He set the record straight with this characteristically modest tale: "I was behind my bar one day in 1944 talking with my bartender, and I told him that I was going to make the finest rum drink in the world. Just then Ham and Carrie Guild, some old friends from Tahiti, came in. Carrie tasted it, raised her glass, and said, 'Mai Tai—Roa Ae,' which in Tahitian means 'Out of this world—the best!' That's the name of the drink, I said, and we named it Mai Tai."

The controversy over who invented the Mai Tai didn't end until Trader Vic took the matter to court, filing a lawsuit against the Sun-Vac Corporation in 1970. By that time, Sun-Vac was licensing a *Don the Beachcomber* line of pre-mixed bottled drink syrups; ironically, Sun-Vac was claiming that it was Don himself—the man Vic freely admitted copying more than thirty years before—who had invented the Mai Tai. The suit was eventually settled out of court in favor of Vic.

"I've sworn at this bar a few times since I built it 35 years ago, so to settle the argument over the origin of the 'Mai Tai' I will swear just once again to get the record straight.

At this bar in 1944 I designed and originated the 'Mai Tai' drink as it is still known and made today ... I served it to my good friends from Tahiti, Ham and Carrie Guild, and asked them to name it."

Trader Vic

Oakland – 1970

"I, too, hereby solemnly swear that on a summer night in 1944 Trader Vic served us a delightfully-flavored drink in an oversized glass filled with fine ice and asked us to suggest an appropriate Tahitian name.

One sip, and my natural reaction was to say 'Mai Tai-Roa Aé', which in Tahitian means 'Out of this world – the best' ... Well, that was that! Vic named the drink 'Mai Tai'."

Carrie Wright

Oakland – 1970

By the 1900s, even the most sophisticated postwar intellectuals were flocking to Tiki bars. Film directors Bob Fosse and Stanley Kubrick were both regulars at the New York *Trader Vic's*—where, in 1964, Kubrick first voiced the idea that four years later would become *2001: A Space Odyssey*.

As the 1970s dawned, popular tastes began to change. Eventually the Missionary's Downfall gave way to the Screaming Orgasm, and the master mixologists of the golden age scattered to the four winds—taking their expertise, experience, and "secret ingredients" with them. Ask today's bartenders to make you a tropical drink, and the sickly sweet results will sadly confirm Tony Ramos's assertion that exotic cocktail mixology is "a lost art."

However, as of this writing there are still a small handful of places that offer the real thing. The *Mai Kai* in Fort Lauderdale, Florida, still serves communal Mystery Drinks in smoking bowls, presented by scantily clad native girls to the sound of a ceremonial gong. And the late Ray Buhen's *Tiki Ti*, now run by his son Mike, is still serving 72 impeccably mixed exotic drinks to the citizens of Los Angeles.

What better way to close this chapter on American alcoholic history than with the words of Ray himself: "It's escapism. It's not real. It's ballyhoo," he said of the faux Polynesian cocktail. And then: "Oh, that was the best time."

WALT DISNEY'S
ENCHANTED TIKI ROOM
A MUSICAL FANTASY WITH AN ASTONISHING CAST
OF AUDIO-ANIMATRONIC PERSONALITIES
AT THE GATEWAY TO
ADVENTURELAN

AND THE GODS WERE AMUSED

Hawaii, 1820, party time. Observing the natives at a hula marathon as they are offering leis (flower garlands) to a god-head, missionary Hiram Bingham tries to understand: "What purpose does your god serve, what is he good for?" Their simple answer puzzles him: "For play!" Incomprehensible to the early 19th-century Puritan, just over a century later this answer was something Americans were ready to understand. Their righteousness and modesty had brought them through the Depression and helped them win the Second World War. Economic security seemed within everyone's grasp and now the time had come to play. But the steadfast morals of the forefathers that constrained this desire were not easily shed. An alternative world had to be created where one could assume a less restrained persona.

The seemingly carefree culture of Polynesia became the escapist counter-reality of choice. Wherever fun could be had, Tiki ruled. Through the multitude of concepts employed to entertain their customers, Tiki bars had already become little amusement parks in themselves. So it was a natural development to integrate Tiki temples into game parks or to create Tiki parks in their own right. The vacation states of California and Florida offered the right combination of recreation-seekers and climate, and so whole Tiki worlds like Tiki Gardens and The Tikis arose. Of course the Big Kahuna of amusement parks, Walt Disney himself,

did not lag behind. A frequent customer in Polynesian supper clubs, he decided to create a Tiki restaurant that would top all existing ones. Walt was an animator, and so to him the logical next step was to make all the usual decor, the flowers, birds, and Tikis come alive. It was the spirit of Tiki that inspired Disney to come up with the concept of "Audio-Animatronics" that later became the heart of many of Disneyland's attractions. But as the project neared completion, the space age technology of 225 robotic performers directed by a fourteen-channel magnetic tape feeding one hundred separate speakers and controlling 438 seperate actions had outgrown the room of the restaurant, and so rather than compromising the complexity of the show, Walt decided to eliminate the restaurant and make the show an attraction in its own right. When "The Enchanted Tiki Room" opened in 1963, the New York Times wrote: "PO-LARIS TAPE AIDS DISNEY ANIMATION—New Synchronizing Device Makes Totem Poles Talk ... In the Enchanted Tiki Room scores of brilliantly colored synthetic birds talk, sing or whistle. Carved pagan gods beat drums and chant in weird syllables. Storms are created and fountains play. Artificial parrots hold conversations in several dialects."

An exalted and rather intellectual review by Stanford professor Don D. Jackson, M. D., Director of the Palo Alto Mental Research Institute, compares the

135

Tiki Room to other man-made power places. Speaking of : "PLAY, PARADOX AND PEOPLE: AWE IN DISNEYLAND," he describes having felt "… as great a sense of awe, wonderment and reverence sitting in the synthetic, fabricated, instant-Polynesian Tiki Room at Disneyland, as I have experienced in some of the great cathedrals – Chartres, Rheims, and Notre Dame …

Another form of family fun center that took up the Tiki theme was the bowling alley. Mostly the adjacent lounges, but sometimes complete establishments, were dedicated to the god of recreation. Bowling originated in German monasteries, where monks had churchgoers knock down a bottle-shaped object known as a *Kegel* to prove their devotion to God. The wooden *Kegel* represented the devil, and upsetting it meant complete absolution from sin. We do not know whether Tiki-shaped bowling pins ever existed, but certainly in many places, aloha shirts and bowling shirts mixed freely while tropical libations steadied the aim of the Tiki revellers.

One such place was the elaborate *Kapu Kai* (or "Forbidden Sea") in Rancho Cucamonga, an obscure suburb of Los Angeles. Four jutting A-frame entrances beckoned the believers. The Tikis stationed around the building and between the lanes were carved by Milan Guanko. His relief Tikis at the entrance door welcomed the arriving devotees with a smile, but frowned on the inside at any deserters. Tiki carpeting lined the floors and the Tahititian Fire Room sported amazing Tapa-cloth fire murals. Still, despite it's inspired designs, the *Kapu Kai* did not survive the end of the 20th century.

HOTEL, MOTEL...

Tourism and Tikis went hand in hand in 1960s America, and since motel signs were the totem poles of American roadside culture, many utilized the Tiki image as attention-getters. Lighthouses in the urban sea, their neon or gas-fed Tiki torches flickered as beacons for weary travellers and modern traders. Polynesia was now reachable by car. The motel was an American mutation of the hotel, created for that four-wheeled holy cow of the car cult, the symbol of progress and prosperity, the American car of the 1950s. The sky was the limit for American car makers in the 50s, the size and design of their products reaching the dimensions of space ships. These hovercrafts needed easy access harbors, with places for their pilots to rest for the next trip. To mark these space ports in the vast urban universe, giant glowing signs were erected by the trade routes.

Thus the motel sign is a classic symbol of Americana culture. It appears a true "sign" of ignorance then that the city of Anaheim, home of Disneyland, which caters to international tourists in search of American pop culture, would destroy motel signs like the *Pit-*

cairn in the course of their "beautification" campaign as recently as 1998. It has been noted that a cultural icon is in it's greatest peril of being destroyed right before it's value gets rediscovered. Consequently we can now look forward to having a bad replica of such signs erected in Disneyland in a couple of years, right next to fake diners equipped with 50's car parts.

The *Hanalei* sign in San Diego is a perfect "Before" and "After" example of corporate ignorance, where for the sake of modernization generic blandness replaces individual expression. Just like the iconographic "Stardust" sign in Las Vegas, it has been replaced with bland Helvetica type which has no connection with the theme.

Yet just as with other Tiki temples, Tiki motels not only flourished in the climatically milder zones, but in other American states as well. The Tiki Motor Inn in Lake George, New York State, had artifical palm trees grouped around the main building which greened even in the snow. As of late this "Oasis of Tropical Splendor" was still in operation, although we cannot say in what condition.

KEN KIMES BUILT
MOTOR HOTELS

But the only true Tiki motel chain arose in the desert cities of California: Ken Kimes once operated forty motels of which five were decked out with Tikis by the craftsmen from Oceanic Arts: The *Tropics* in Indio, Blythe, Rosemead, Modesto and Palm Springs. Four of them still feature Tikis that have fared well in their dry climate. The Palm Springs *Tropics* is the most elaborate, although the *Reef* bar has recently been renovated in the Mexican motif. Hopefully the rediscovery of Palm Springs as a hub of mid-century modernism will aid the preservation of this rare Tiki Temple.

Really live it up at the *tropics*

UNEQUALLED IN BACHELOR LIVING

"… cross the hand-carved footbridge above the fiery pit of the goddess PELE, where the lava is about to boil and the land is about to tremble, then you're in the region supreme over all—a domain far from stresses, cares and worries, yet merely minutes from public transportation, churches and just seconds from the mainland … In this fantastic setting, PELE knows all. She has been, and shall always be, in the pantheon of Hawaiian worship. You will relax and lounge in the sun around the palm-studded swimming area with the flowing waters of the coral fountain falling into the beautifully contoured lagoon. On the inside footbridge you will find yourself amidst the ruins of her domain, where the remains of Hopoe and Lohiau have been transformed into two large rocks in the turbulent waters cascading down the lava-covered side of a seething volcano. Here, within the Consolation of the Gods, you can make your home, live among the beautiful palms in a setting unequalled in bachelor living … Just pick up your key and become another of the inhabitants of this exotic little village in the center a bustling city."

This evocative example of Polynesian pop poetry from the brochure of the *Pele* Apartments gives an idea of the pains developers went through to create these "Polynesian" settlements of the targeted recreation seekers. The architectural concepts employed all hailed from Tiki restaurants and lounges, and in the unique case of the *Pele* Apartments, even

ESCAPE TO **PARADISE**

LIVE LIKE AN ISLANDER

VISIT

(GODDESS OF FIRE)

the typeface and liner notes of a popular Exotica album were copied as well.

Another fine concept of apartment living was realized by the same developer at the *Shelter Isle* apartment complex, whose advertising text foreshadowed the demise of its own culture twenty years later: "As one leaves the recreation area and leisurely meanders along the winding pathways he suddenly finds himself amidst the ruins of an abandoned village. Here the remains of a native settlement stand lonely beside a small lake fed by turbulent waters cascading down the lava-covered sides of a seething volcano."

Tiki villages (Polynesian apartment complexes) today provide the Tiki cultural archeologist with a more rewarding environment, having survived the abolishment of idolatry better then their progenitors, the Tiki temples (restaurants and lounges). Not as dependent on changes in taste as the restaurant industry, these villages sometimes represent virtual sanctuaries of that endangered species, the Tiki.

Although some owners and managers have tried with missionary zeal to "update" such sites, and many Tikis have rotted away or been stolen by grave robbers, scanning the urban sea of L. A. for tall palm trees and A-frame structures can still yield spectacular discoveries. At the *Tahitian Village* in the San Fernando Valley, two Gauguinesque native sculptures flanking the entrance bridge represent the archetypes of fire and water. Water once spouted from the mouth of the male, then fell into his hands, and emptied into the moat under the bridge, while the female held an open gas flame in her hand.

Like the temples, the villages were most widespread in California and by no means limited to its warmer climes. All the way up the West Coast, around the Seattle area, in Tacoma and Bremerton, a Navy shipyard town, numerous Tiki dwellings sprang up. All across America, more or less elaborate communities formed to hail the godhead of recreation. The names of these suburban islands were as evocative as their type styles. From the "Beachcomber," "Asian," "Primitive," and "Bamboo" to the "Fat Samoan" style, they all represented elements of the Tiki esthetic. Some of the wings or sections of the apartments had their own designations like "Snug Harbor" or "Mauna Loa," taken from Hawaiian sites or hotels.

The *Exotic Isle* Apartments in the Los Angeles suburb of Alhambra, which was named after the Moorish palace in Spain and is now mostly inhabited by Asian immigrants, was until very recently another impressive manifestation of the Tiki faith. Its centerpiece is a recreation room jutting out over the central waterfall, a structure which could be seen as the Tiki equivalent of Frank Lloyd Wright's "Falling Water."

155

BACKYARD POLYNESIA

In more ways than one, the average American's desire to "go native" was a regression to a simpler period of life: childhood. The responsibilities of work and family were best forgotten at luau-themed garden parties—a sort of "big guys" birthday party—where fun and games were once more allowed. Donning flowery Hawaiian shirts and "muu muus," consuming sweet foods and sweeter drinks that lowered the intellect to child-like consciousness, white grown-ups spent their time Hula dancing and practicing the consonantless sing-song of the Hawaiian language: "All KANES, WAHINES and KEIKIS (men, women and children) will want to

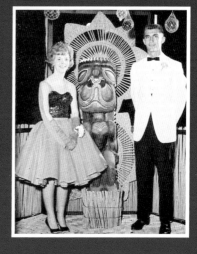

WIKI WIKI (hurry) to a Hawaiian LUAU (feast). MALIHINIS (newcomers) will want to know the meaning of the strange words they confront at a luau. Wahines will wear HOLOKUS (Hawaiian princess dresses with a train) or MUU MUUS [loose-fitting flowered garment]. Kanes will wear ALOHA shirts (brightly-colored sport shirts). No PAPALE (hat) is needed. ALOHA (greetings) will be expressed by placing a LEI (flower wreath) about the neck of the malihini. The luau will be served on long tables placed on a LANAI (open porch) or under palm frond awnings in the yard. The luau food is cooked in an IMU (under-

ground oven) made by digging a LUA (hole) in the ground, filling it with POHAKU (rocks) and KUNI (kindling).

Imu holes were dug in backyards as if the gold rush days had returned, but the pure desire to go primitive was not enough. Appropriate decor was needed. The necessary paraphenalia to equip these happenings could be found at nurseries and specialty stores like "Sea and Jungle" in the Valley, "Oceanic Arts" in Whittier, and "Johnson Products" in Chicago. Tiki torches, grass matting, palm leaves, bamboo poles, fish netting, spears and drums, and Tiki-shaped items could be found at these suppliers. Thus Tiki huts appeared in backyards and god-

heads were erected by pools and patios, making Tikis the new garden gnomes of America.

For the hobbist, there were complete kits with instructions on how to build one's own Tiki bar. In many suburban homes, the basements were turned into rumpus rooms where grown-ups would gather for cocktails and adult talk. When rattan and bamboo furniture did not impress enough, Tiki-carved bars and chairs from the house of Witco did the trick.

Always a good parameter of popular taste, Elvis Presley equipped his Jungle Room in Graceland with Witco furnishings.

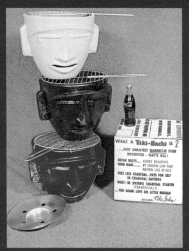

The creators of the unrecognized art form of Tiki-moderne, American Tiki sculptors, have never been accepted as artists. Their products were labeled "authentic," a shadowy term denoting genuineness, but not outright claiming that the works were originals. Nobody wanted to draw attention to the fact that the dark complexion of a carver like Vince Buono, for example, derived from his New York Italian immigrant background and not from the South Sea Isles. Tiki style did not seek to betray intentionally; rather, it gently supported the public's need for self-deception, and therefore cloaked itself and its creators in mystery. The power tool Leroy Schmaltz is swinging on this page was taboo at public carving appearances, where hammer and chisel were used. This chapter aims to give several Tiki artists—representative for all who could not be included here—their due recognition.

Leroy Schmaltz and Bob van Oosting founded their decorating firm, Oceanic Arts, in the Los Angeles suburb of Whittier in the late 1950s, just on the crest of the Tiki craze. Beginning on a

small scale with Tiki amulets and palm frond masks, Oceanic Arts soon emerged as *the* major manufacturer and supplier countrywide of Tiki art and materials. Schmaltz and van Oosting were contracted by all the major chains, from *Don the Beachcomber* to *Kon-Tiki*; in turn, they themselves employed most of the carvers in the business at one point or another. Occasionally the Tikis were designed by the architects or decorators who commissioned them, but mostly the sculptors pursued their own visions, and sometimes became the designers of the Tiki environments, as well.

The list of credits collected by Oceanic Arts is extensive: they have been connected with most of the Tiki temples depicted in this book. Even the honorable Bishop Museum in Honolulu houses some of their carvings—if not in museum display cases, at least on the walls of its cafeteria. The phenomenon of the Tiki style went full circle when idols man-ufactured by Oceanic Arts were exported to hotels and restaurants in Hawaii, Samoa and Tahiti. Today, Oceanic Arts is the only Polynesian supplier of Tiki decor; having suc-cessfully survived the abolishment of Tiki, they are now beckoning a new generation of explorers from all over the world to the shores of Whittier, California.

Just across the Golden Gate bridge north of San Francisco, in the quaint yacht harbor of Sausalito, ex-merchant marine Barney West set up camp with his Tiki Junction. He had found his vocation during the Second World War when he was stranded in the Mariana Islands. His Tiki Junction logo was inspired by a book published in conjunction with the first exhibition of South Seas art in America in 1946, the same source that also spawned the Trader Vic logo. Trader Vic, based across the bay in Emeryville, near Oakland, be-came the main purchaser of Barney's Tikis. Today some of these effigies bearing his un-mistakable style can still be found in Trader Vic's franchises all around the world. Mean-while Barney, who fully fit the role of the hard-drinking, womanizing bohemian, has long since gone to Tiki heaven.

Milan Guanko learned carving as a child from his father in the Philippines. After emi-grating to the States in 1928 and working in groceries, he found his niche in the emerg-ing Polynesian craze. Eventually becoming one of the most prolif-ic and influential Tiki carvers in America, his style was copied and marketed for the growing needs of Tiki revellers. His credits include pieces at *The Islands* in Phoenix, Arizona; the *Kapu Kai* in Rancho Cucamonga; and Ren Clark's *Polynesian Village* in Fort Worth, Texas, for which Guanko and two Mexican carvers, Juan Razo and Fidel Rodriguez (who had also outfitted the *Mauna Loa* in Mexico City), carved over two hundred Tikis, some as barstools, some as 11-foot-tall giants. A state-of-the-art Polynesian par-adise in 1960, nothing remains today of this virtual forest of Tikis, the whereabouts of its many erstwhile inhabitants being un-known.

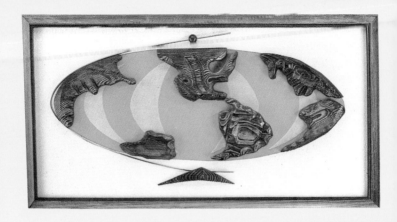

In William Westenhaver's world of Witco, only a carved piece of wood was a good piece of wood. Be it in his "burnt wood relief on shag carpet" paintings or complete "primitive bedroom" sets, no smooth surface escaped the chainsaw of this mad genius. Wherever a Tiki face could be applied, wood shavings flew. Then the carving was burnished with a torch to bring out the grain structure of the wood in thick black veins. Not only Poly-

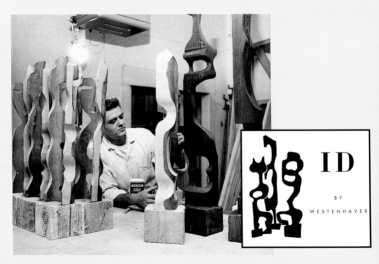

...nesian art, but also modern and Conquistador decor was churned and burned at the Witco plant in Seattle. At one time Witco had showrooms in Chicago, Dallas, Denver, and Seattle. Westenhaver's art can still be found in Florida motels as well as in thrift stores throughout the U. S. His list of customers included Elvis Presley and Hugh Hefner. Even several houses of ill repute are rumored to have been clients. Among his most distinguished works are a variety of Tiki bars and Tiki fountains. The author is presently working on a monograph on the œuvre of this prolific whittler, hoping that this first book will have opened the eyes of the public to the art of Tiki.

TIKI STYLE. DER KULT DES POLY-NEOIOCHEN POP IM AMERIKA DER FÜNFZIGER JAHRE

EIN FÜHRER FÜR DEN STADTARCHÄOLOGEN. DIE ENTDECKUNG EINER VERLORENEN ZIVILISATION VOR UNSERER EIGENEN HAUSTÜR

„Die Krankheit der Holzfäulnis verbreitet sich unter den Idolen, die Früchte auf ihren Altären sind nicht mehr wohlgefällig, selbst die Tempel sollten neu gedeckt werden …"
(Herman Melville: Taipi, 1846)
Diese Bemerkung über das Schicksal der alten polynesischen Zivilisation stammt zwar aus einem Klassiker der Südseeliteratur, scheint jedoch auch auf das Schicksal des amerikanischen Tiki-Stils der 50er und 60er Jahre auf befremdliche Weise zuzutreffen. Seine Symbole, die Tikis, verfallen, die „polynesische" Küche jener Zeit gilt heute als das genaue Gegenteil einer gesunden Ernährung, und die wenigen noch existierenden Zeugnisse der Tiki-Architektur sehen baufällig aus. Schon Paul Gauguin war fasziniert von der melancholischen Atmosphäre des Zerfalls in Papeete, Tahitis Hauptstadt, als er die „verschwommene Oberfläche eines unergründlichen Rätsels" in diesem bereits befleckten Paradies entdeckte; ebenso ergeht es dem Stadtarchäologen von heute, der die Überreste jenes „verlorenen Paradieses", jener amerikanischen Version des Dolce Vita, die wir Tiki-Stil nennen, betrachtet.
Tiki-Tempel, die einst jede größere amerikanische Stadt zierten, sind verschwunden oder umgestaltet worden, die „unbeholfenen, lustig aussehenden Götzenbilder" (Melville) hat man mit missionarischem Eifer hinausgeworfen, um neuen Göttern oder Stilen Platz zu machen. Wasserfälle haben aufgehört zu fließen – ebenso wie die übernatürliche Kraft des „Mana", mit dem sie erbaut wurden; die Tiki-Fackeln sind erloschen und die Auslegerbalken sind abgesägt.
Aber die Stadtarchäologen haben eine Sensibilität für verlorene Kulturen und ihre vergessenen Sitten und Gebräuche entwickelt. Unerschrocken reisen sie zu ihren „Grabungsstätten" an so entlegenen und exotischen Orten wie Columbus, Ohio, oder Pomona im städtischen Einzugsgebiet von Los Angeles. Für sie ist es ebenso aufregend, an einem Tag voller Smog über eine öde Schnellstraße in irgendeinen auf keiner Karte verzeichneten Vorort eines

Vorortes zu fahren, wie das „Kon-Tiki" durch einen Hurrikan im Pazifik zu steuern. Wie „Stadtstreicher" im wahrsten Sinne des Wortes durchwühlen sie die Abfälle der Konsumkultur, in Secondhandläden, bei Hinterhofverkäufen und in Antiquariaten, immer auf der Suche nach Puzzlesteinen zu jener versunkenen Kultur, die polynesische Paradiese inmitten der Städte entstehen ließ. Mit seinem wachen Sinn für das Wunderbare erkennt der Stadtarchäologe, dass man nicht immer in die Ferne schweifen muss, um die Geheimnisse vergessener, uralter Traditionen zu erforschen, sondern dass fremdartige Schätze in der unmittelbaren Nachbarschaft begraben liegen können. Das ist es, was wir uns mit diesem Buch, Ihrem Führer zur Tiki-Kultur in Amerika, vorgenommen haben: die Fähigkeit zu erwecken, das Wunderbare im scheinbar so Profanen zu entdecken.

AM ANFANG WAR …

Seit dem Sündenfall hat der Mensch immer danach gestrebt, wieder in das Paradies zurückzukehren, aus dem er vertrieben worden ist. Als die ersten Berichte von den Südseeinseln die Alte Welt erreichten, glaubte man, diesen wiederentdeckt zu haben. Polynesien wurde zur Metapher für das Paradies auf Erden – dessen Strände blieben allerdings für die meisten Sterblichen unerreichbar und so ging die Suche nach anderen mythischen Ländern weiter. Ein solches Land war „California", eine mysteriöse Insel, die man für einen ganzen Kontinent hielt und von der gesagt wurde, dass sie von Amazonen bevölkert sei. Obwohl diese Terra incognita bald besiedelt wurde und derartige Höhenflüge der Fantasie sich als Übertreibung herausstellten, behielt Kalifornien immer seinen Status als goldenes Traumziel. Generationen von Menschen kamen hier an, alle auf der Suche nach der Verwirklichung ihrer eigenen Vorstellung vom Paradies. Eine der vielen Versionen dieses Glücks auf Erden war der tropische Garten der Südseeinseln, und so kam es, dass die erste Palme gepflanzt wurde und sich eine tropische Flora ausbreitete. Da nicht nur die Biosphäre, sondern auch die entsprechende Psycho-Sphäre vorhanden war, bildete sich schon bald ein amerikanisches Polynesien heraus. Tiki-Tempel wurden gebaut und eine Zeit lang waren die Menschen gläubig. Sie kamen zusammen, um dem Kult der modernen Primitivismus zu huldigen, einem Kult, in den die Alkoholismus, Rassismus, Chauvinismus und Schweinefleischverzehr integriert waren – heute absolute Tabus.
Wie die Kalifornier Polynesien nachahmten, so schaute der Rest der Nation auf Ka-

lifornien, um von dort etwas über neue Lebensstile zu erfahren. Schon bald verfügte jede größere Stadt in Amerika über zumindest einen polynesischen Palast.

TIKI – WER WAR DAS?

Am Anfang war das Wort und das Wort lautete: TIK, zumindest nach Angaben des renommierten Spracharchäologen und Linguisten Merrit Ruhlen aus Palo Alto, Kalifornien. Er verfolgte den Ursprung der menschlichen Sprache bis auf dieses magische Dreibuchstabenwort zurück, das sich noch heute in „toe" (Zeh), in „digit" (Finger) und offensichtlich auch in „dick" (Schwanz) erhalten hat. Wenn „Tiki" mit soviel archaischer Kraft ausgestattet ist, darf man sich nicht wundern, dass es zum Schlagwort einer ganzen Generation geworden ist.
Aber „Tiki" weist nicht nur diese enge Verwandtschaft mit dem ersten Wort auf, sondern ist in der polynesischen Mythologie auch das Synonym für den ersten Menschen. Schlägt man in A. W. Reeds „Concise Maori Dictionary" nach, findet man die folgenden Erklärungen:
1. TIKI: Erster Mensch oder Personifizierung des Menschen. Durch Ahnenverehrung wurde dieser Maori-Adam zu einem Halbgott und schließlich wurde der Begriff „Tiki" für alle Darstellungen des Menschen verwendet, wie im zweiten Bedeutungsfeld erörtert:
2. TIKI: Groteske Schnitzerei in menschlicher Gestalt an einem Haus – eine präzise Beschreibung der Art von Tiki, wie man ihn auf diesen Seiten finden. Lesen wir aber weiter, zeigt sich eine noch tiefere Bedeutung des Wortes:
3. TIKI: ein phallisches Symbol. Tatsächlich ist Tiki in den Überlieferungen der Maori der Name für die Zeugungskraft und das Sexualorgan des Gottes Tane, des Schöpfers der ersten Frau. Auf den Tuban-Inseln südlich von Tahiti war „Tiki-roa" (die lange Ahnengestalt) der Spitzname für den Penis und „Tiki-poto" (die kurze Ahnengestalt) ein Kosewort für die Klitoris.
Da das Wort so schöpferische Kräfte in sich trägt, wird es niemanden überraschen, auf den Marquesa-Inseln noch eine weitere Bedeutung zu finden:
4. TIKI: Gott der Künstler. Es ist ein Anliegen dieses Buches zu zeigen, dass Tiki tatsächlich die Muse vieler Künstler war, ob bekannter oder unbekannter. Möge er sich nun auch als der lang ersehnte Schirmherr der Künstler etablieren.

PRIMITIVE KUNST AN ZIVILISIERTEN ORTEN

„Wer sie je gesehen hat, fühlt sich von ihnen verfolgt wie von einem Fieberträum."

(Karl Woermann über Tikis in seiner *Geschichte der Kunst aller Zeiten und Völker*, 1900–1911)

Die scheinbar naive und ursprüngliche Ästhetik der so genannten primitiven Kunst diente den Urvätern der modernen Kunst als entscheidende Inspirationsquelle – in diesen Anfängen gründet das Prinzip, später diese primitive Kunst in Kontrast zu den glatten Linien des modernen Designs zu setzen, um dessen Wirkung zu verstärken. Im frühen 20. Jahrhundert kamen immer mehr „Kunstkuriositäten", also afrikanische und ozeanische Kunstobjekte, aus den Kolonien in die westeuropäischen Großstädte; eine junge Künstlergeneration, zu der Pablo Picasso, Joan Miró, Paul Klee und Max Ernst gehörten, benutzte den Primitivismus, um den bis dahin gültigen Kunstbegriff in Frage zu stellen. Das Studium der etablierten klassischen Kunst, sagte Gauguin damals, „stieß mich ab und entmutigte mich, denn es gab mir so ein unbestimmtes Gefühl, zu sterben, ohne wieder geboren zu werden". Pablo Picasso hatte sein Erweckungserlebnis, als er die Sammlung primitiver Kunst im Musée d'Ethnographie du Trocadéro in Paris sah: „Plötzlich wusste ich, warum ich Maler geworden war!" Schon 1919 wurde er als „alter Anhänger von Tiki" begrüßt. Das lag wahrscheinlich daran, dass Picasso schon um 1910 stolzer Besitzer eines Tiki von den Marquesa-Inseln war, von dem er sich für den Rest seiner einzigartigen Karriere nicht mehr trennte.

Während die primitive Kunst in den 20er und 30er Jahren vorwiegend von der Avantgarde geschätzt wurde, interessierte sich nach dem Zweiten Weltkrieg auch der wohlhabende Mittelstand für diese Objekte: Man verband mit ihnen einen künstlerischen, bohemehaften Lebensstil und eine originelle, spielerische Lebenseinstellung. In den späten 50er Jahren war es ein absolutes Muss, irgendeine hinreißende Plastik aus dem Busch zu besitzen und so die Monotonie der damaligen Wohnzimmereinrichtungen ein wenig aufzulockern. Die Zeit des Tiki war gekommen.

PRÄ-TIKI UND DIE GEBURT DES POLYNESISCHEN POP

„Man sollte oft wünschen, auf einer der Südseeinseln als so genannter Wilder geboren zu sein, um nur einmal das menschliche Dasein ohne falschen Beigeschmack, durchaus rein zu genießen." (Goethe zu Eckermann, 12.3.1828). Der Wunsch, die Segnungen der Zivilisation gegen ein einfacheres, natürliches Leben einzutauschen, ist so alt wie die Zivilisation selbst. Eskapistische Träumer und ernsthafte Philosophen waren der Ansicht, dass in den frühen Reiseberichten von den Südsee-Expeditionen James Cooks und Louis-Antoine de Bougainvilles die perfekte Alternative zu den Lebensbedingungen der affektierten Gesellschaft im alten Europa beschrieben sei. Melville pries in „Taipi" die Natürlichkeit der eingeborenen Mädchen: „Ich hätte gern für einen Augenblick eine Galerie Krönungsschönheiten aus Westminster/Abbey dieser Schar Inselmädchen gegenübergestellt, ihre Steifheit, Förmlichkeit und Geziertheit mit der ungekünstelten Lebhaftigkeit und der unverhüllten natürlichen Anmut dieser wilden Geschöpfe verglichen."

Angenehmes Klima, natürliche Schönheit, leidenschaftliche Eingeborene und exotische Nahrungsmittel im Überfluss versprachen ein Leben frei von allen Einschränkungen und Belastungen der modernen westlichen Gesellschaft. Abenteuergeschichten über Polynesien wurden so populär, dass 1921 bei G. P. Putnam's Sons eine Parodie auf derartige Südsee-Expeditionen mit dem Titel „The Cruise of the Kawa" herauskam. Obwohl das Werk schon durch seine Fotos eindeutig als Satire erkennbar war, erwies sich die Nachfrage nach dieser Art von literarischer Kost als so groß, dass man die Berichte als authentisch betrachtete und der Autor sogar zu einem Vortrag vor der National Geographic Society eingeladen wurde. Wenn es um die Darstellung des Paradieses auf Erden ging, war man nur allzu leicht geneigt, der Fiktion gegenüber den nüchternen Tatsachen den Vorzug zu geben. Mit diesem Buch etablierte sich auch der Sinn fürs Humorvolle, der von da an den polynesischen Pop beherrschte. Ursprünglich aber waren es viel archaischere Bedürfnisse, die durch die Berichte aus Polynesien angesprochen worden waren. „Auf der Insel Otaheite (Tahiti), wo Liebe die Hauptbeschäftigung ist, der bevorzugte Luxus, oder genauer gesagt, der einzige Luxus der Einwohner, sind die Körper und Seelen der Frauen perfekt geformt." (Joseph Banks, 1743–1820, Naturforscher auf Cooks „Endeavour"). Bemerkungen wie diese machten uns den nackten Eingeborenenmädchen, der Wahine, die Eva im polynesischen Garten Eden. Sie wurde die erste und wichtigste Ikone des polynesischen Pop, verkörperte sie doch die Verheißung bedingungsloser Liebe. Bald kamen andere Sinnbilder hinzu, zum Beispiel die Palme, die Eingeborenenhütte, das Einbaumkanu und alle Arten exotischer Tiere und Pflanzen, die eine ganze Galerie populärer Symbole der ozeanischen Kultur bildeten. Tiki war bislang lediglich eine von vielen Figuren, die das Märchenland „Polynesia-Americana" bevölkerten.

Als in den 20er Jahren im ganzen Land eine riesige Begeisterung für hawaiische Musik ausbrach, wurde auch die Hawaiigitarre, die Ukulele, immer beliebter. Nachtclubs rissen sich um hawaiische Entertainer und die Clubs legten sich zunehmend ein tropisches Ambiente zu. Bambus und Rattan vom Boden bis zur Decke, üppige tropische Pflanzen und Wandschmuck von den Inseln gehörten für diese frühen Stadtflüchtigen zur Grundausstattung, mit der sie sich die Illusion verschafften, in die Südsee entkommen zu sein.

Und bald richtete sich die allgemeine Aufmerksamkeit auf ein neues Symbol: In Europa entstanden die ersten Zoos und zu ihrer Attraktionen wurden auch „wirkliche Wilde" hinzugenommen, *das* Faszinosum für die Damenwelt, worüber sich die Journalisten immer wieder mokierten. Das ambivalente Verhältnis von Attraktion und Aversion, mit dem man den „Wilden" begegnete, die Anziehungskraft des „exotischen Anderen" fand Eingang in das kollektive Bewusstsein der westlichen Welt. In der Polynesischen Popkultur nahm diese Faszination die Form des Tiki an.

TIKI: EINE GENERATION SPANNT AUS

„Das ganze Wesen der Götzenanbetung, welches von einem Volk gepflegt wurde, das von der Mehrheit seiner Artgenossen durch das unendliche Meer getrennt war, aber in ungewöhnlichen Masse über die Mittel verfügte, sich nicht nur selbst zu erhalten, sondern sogar im Überfluss zu leben, ist eine höchst bewegende Zurschaustellung von Dummheit, Absurdität und Entwürdigung." (Reverend William Ellis: Polynesian Researches, 1831). In den 50er Jahren waren die Amerikaner bereit, die Früchte ihrer harten Arbeit, die ihnen wirtschaftliche Unabhängigkeit und Wohlstand gebracht hatte, zu ernten. Sie waren als Helden aus dem Zweiten Weltkrieg hervorgegangen und sonnten sich in internationalem Erfolg und Anerkennung. Doch dasselbe puritanische Arbeitsethos, durch das sie es so weit gebracht hatten, zog auch ein ganzes Bündel sozialer und moralischer Einschränkungen nach sich, die es ihnen erschwerten, ihren Wohlstand zu genießen.

Polynesische Partys gestatteten dem Mann im grauen Flanellanzug, sich in einen von allen Regeln befreiten Wilden zu verwandeln: In bunte Hawaii-Hemden gekleidet (die nicht in die Hose gesteckt werden mussten), leicht berauscht von exotischen Drinks mit noch exotischeren Namen, die an Babysprache erinnerten (Lapu Lapu, Mauna Loa Puki), während sie mit bloßen Händen von dem Luau-Schwein

165

aßen und sich an Hula- und Limbo-Wettbewerben beteiligten – endlich durften sie sich vergnügen und sich gehen lassen, und das in einer Gesellschaft, in der es ansonsten ausgesprochen konservativ zu ging.

Eine weitere Freiheit, die man als „Vorstadtwilder" genoss, war die Erlaubnis, sich Bilder von barbusigen eingeborenen Frauen anzusehen, solange dies etwas mit einem anthropologischen Interesse zu tun hatte, man also eine Art National Geographic-Erotik praktizierte. Doch als die Wahine und all die anderen Klischee-Ikonen des Südsee-Märchenlandes wieder hervorgeholt wurden, tauchte eine neue Gallionsfigur des polynesischen Volksbrauchtums auf: das geschnitzte Götzenbild der Eingeborenen, das gemeinhin Tiki genannt wurde. Obwohl es diesen Begriff weder in der hawaiischen noch in tahitischen Sprache gab und die Steinskulpturen auf den Osterinseln immer noch „Moai" hießen, wurden im polynesischen Pop alle ozeanischen Schnitzereien Mitglieder einer großen glücklichen Familie: der Tikis. Diese primitiven Götzen waren ein Antidot gegen die moderne Welt aus Plastik und Chrom, phallische Monumente der menschlichen Triebe. Zwar richteten sich die amerikanischen Tikis in ihrer Form weitgehend nach ihren polynesischen Vorbildern, waren aber doch meistens frei nachempfundene Interpretationen von Stilen, die sich aus mehreren Inselkulturen zusammensetzten, gemischt mit einer guten Dosis Comics-Fantasie und einem Touch moderner Kunst. Selbst die Figuren, die als „authentisch" bezeichnet werden konnten, waren lediglich Kopien von den wenigen Originalen, die den fanatischen „Bildersturm" der Missionare überlebt hatten. Diese liberale Einstellung gegenüber Nachbildungen hatte sich auf den hawaiischen Inseln schon bei den frühesten westlichen Kontakten abgezeichnet, wie man aus dem folgenden Dokument von 1825 ersieht: „Die Offiziere des königlich britannischen Schiffes ‚Blonde' wollten, als sie sich hier aufhielten, unbedingt ein paar alte Götzenbilder haben, um sie als Andenken mit nach Hause zu nehmen. Durch die große Nachfrage waren die verfügbaren Vorräte bald erschöpft: Um den Mangel zu beheben, fertigten die Hawaiianer neue Figuren und schwärzten sie mit Rauch, um ihnen ein antikes Aussehen zu geben, und tatsächlich gelang ihnen diese Täuschung." (W. S. W. Ruschenberger: Extracts from the Journal of an American Naval Officer, 1841). Mehr als ein Jahrhundert später erklärte nicht nur Pablo Picasso, ein Sammler primitiver Kunst und begeisterter Flohmarktbesucher: „Man braucht kein Meisterwerk, um

die Idee zu verstehen. Die Grundidee oder das Wesentliche eines Stils wird auch bei einem zweitklassigen Exemplar und sogar bei Fälschungen völlig plausibel." Also hatten auch amerikanische Künstler, die ganz vom Geist des Tiki erfüllt waren, keine Hemmungen, die Götzenköpfe auf ihre bizarre Art neu zu kreieren.

Ein perfektes Beispiel für diesen Stil ist der Tiki, den Alec Yuill-Thornton für Tiki Bob's Bar in San Francisco schuf. Diese Skulptur, ein bisschen George Jetson, ein bisschen moderner Primitivismus, hat nur noch sehr wenig mit den ozeanischen Artefakten zu tun. Sie markiert aber, gemeinsam mit dem Tiki-Signet von Stephen Cranes Luau den Beginn des Tiki-Stils. Zum ersten Mal wurde ein Tiki als Logo verwendet; er stand als Wächter am Eingang, war auf den Speisekarten und Streichholzheftchen abgebildet und tauchte auch als Krug und als Salz- und Pfefferstreuer wieder auf.

„Sneaky" Bob Bryant hatte als Trader Vics Barkeeper gearbeitet, aber als sie sich 1955 überwarfen, zog Bob vom Traders am Cosmo Place einen Block weiter und eröffnete eine eigene Bar. Sein Versuch, dieses Konzept als Franchise an das Capitol Inn in Sacramento zu verkaufen, hatte nur kurzfristigen Erfolg. Bob eröffnete außerdem Tiki Bobs Mainland an der Bush Street, wo er Dessous-Modenschauen veranstaltete, um die Geschäftsleute zur Mittagszeit anzulocken.

Tiki wurde zum Star im polynesischen Pop-Theater und so taufte man mit seinem Namen viele Lokale quer durch die U. S. A., von Alabama bis Alaska, wobei er in seinen vielfältigen Erscheinungsformen unzählige Bars schmückte, die den zivilisationsmüden Zeitgenossen Erfrischung versprachen. Tiki-Darstellungen erreichten den Höhepunkt ihrer Beliebtheit, als in der TV-Serie „Hawaiian Eye" ein Tiki als Logo benutzt wurde; diese Serie wurde von 1959 bis 1963 ausgestrahlt, und das archaische Logo grub sich fast unmerklich in die hypnotisierten Mittelstandsgemüter ein.

Aber als das Tiki-Fieber gerade auf seinem Höhepunkt angekommen war, setzte ihm der schwere Generationenkonflikt der 60er Jahre ein Ende. Die Kinder der Tiki-Schwärmer beschlossen, sich ihr eigenes Nirwana zu erschaffen, wo die freie Liebe und exotisches Glück zur Realität wurden. Alkohol gehörte nicht länger zu den bevorzugten Rauschmitteln, Marihuana und psychedelische Drogen wurden zum neuen Freizeitvergnügen, und gleichzeitig schien die sexuelle Revolution alle puritanischen Begriffe von Monogamie hinwegzufegen. Die tropischen Cocktails gerieten ebenso in Konflikt mit dem wachsenden Gesund-

heitsbewusstsein wie die fettige und süße pseudo-chinesische Küche.

Die „britische Invasion" verlagerte das Interesse der jungen Generation auf einen weiteren merkwürdigen Kult aus Übersee: The Beatles. Und in ihrem Song „Holiday in Waikiki" klagten The Kings über ein Plastikpolynesien: „... and even all the grass skirts were PVC!" Genau wie die Polynesier zwei Jahrhunderte zuvor festgestellt hatten, dass die weißen Forscher keine Götter waren, als sie Captain Cook in einem Scharmützel in der Kealakekua Bay töten konnten, erlebten die Amerikaner mit dem Kennedy-Attentat 1963 einen traumatischen Zusammenbruch ihres Selbstbewusstseins. Das war der Anfang vom Ende, der Verlust ihrer jungenhaften Unschuld, sowohl in der Selbstwahrnehmung als auch in dem Bild, das die Welt von Amerika hatte.

Exotica und Tiki-Style wurden als Rituale denunziert, die vom imperialistischen Establishment erfunden worden seien, und das zu einer Zeit, da die Erkenntnis sich durchzusetzen begann, dass der Vietnamkrieg von Beginn an ein grauenvoller Fehler gewesen war – sah man doch im Fernsehen Eingeborenenhütten und Palmen brennen. Junge Rebellen zogen im Protestmarsch zum Capitol in Washington, während Richard Nixon in seinem Stammlokal, dem Washington Trader Vic's, Mai-Tais schlürfte.

Zusätzlich wurde der für die jüngere Generation diskreditierte polynesische Stil in den 70er Jahren durch die Einführung eines generalisierten Tropenthemas verwässert, das keine eindeutige Identität, keine Inselmerkmale mehr aufwies. Ob Karibik, Mexiko oder Polynesien, überall war „Margharita-Ville". Die populäre Fernsehshow „Fantasy Island" war ein typisches Beispiel für diese politisch korrekte Abgrenzung von kultureller Komplizenschaft und kreierte stattdessen eine Welt im Kolonialstil aus Korbgeflecht, durchmischt mit exotischen Pflanzen. Die mit Farnen dekorierte Bar trat nun an die Stelle der Tiki-Bar.

Die 80er Jahre waren das Jahrzehnt des Niedergangs der Tiki-Kultur. Die polynesischen Paläste wurden entweder dem Erdboden gleichgemacht oder so umgebaut, dass man sie nicht wieder erkannte; sie verschwanden, ohne dass man sie je als eine besondere Facette der amerikanischen Popkultur anerkannt hatte. In den 80er Jahren stellten sie nur noch eine peinliche Geschmacksverirrung dar. Unbemerkt und unbetrauert verschwand eine ganze kulturelle Tradition.

DER BAU EINES TIKI-TEMPELS

Der Bau eines „Hale Tiki" (Tiki-Hauses) war ein kompliziertes Unterfangen, nicht nur wegen der diversen exotischen Materialien, die dafür benötigt wurden, sondern auch wegen der außergewöhnlichen Entwürfe, mit denen man die Tiki-Anhänger, die sich hier exotischen Trinkritualen hingaben, verblüffen und begeistern wollte. Dieses Kapitel möchte einen bisher kaum gewürdigten Aspekt der amerikanischen Popkultur vorstellen und befaßt sich mit den für den Tiki-Stil charakteristischen architektonischen Ausdrucksformen. Obwohl es eine klare Traditionslinie gibt, der man sich seit *Don the Beachcomber* anschloss und man bestimmte Entwürfe immer und immer wieder aufgriff und variierte, so ist es doch kennzeichnend für den Tiki-Stil, dass jin jeder, der vom Tiki-Fieber erfasst war, auf seine Weise neu interpretierte. Vom künstlichen Dschungel bis zu bestimmten Ritualen, mit denen die Drinks serviert wurden, die Fantasie kannte keine Grenzen, als die Amerikaner einmal beschlossen hatten, dem Ruf von Tiki zu folgen und ihre ganz persönlichen Versionen eines Südsee-Refugiums zu entwerfen.

Der beliebteste architektonische Entwurf war der einer A-Form. War es bloßer Zufall, dass gegen Ende der 50er Jahre der neue Primitivismus des Tiki-Stils auf sein genaues Gegenteil traf, den futuristischen Stil des Düsenzeitalters, oder bedingte das eine das andere? Wie auch immer, beide vereinten sich ruhmvoll unter der A-Form. Mit Eero Saarinens TWA-Terminal und Frank Lloyd Wrights First Unitarian Church wurden spitz aufragende Giebel zum Lieblingsspielzeug moderner Architekten. Wie in der Heckflosse des Cadillac drückte sich auch in ihm der optimistische Glaube an das Raketenzeitalter aus.

Zufällig waren die meisten traditionellen ozeanischen Wohnhäuser Palmenhütten und daher in A-Form errichtet. Doch da die Eingeborenenhäuser der Polynesier mit Ausnahme der kunstvoll geschnitzten Maori-Versammlungshäuser gänzlich ungeschmückt waren, bediente man sich der Südseekultur. Das neuguineische Kulthaus oder „Haus Tambaran" mit seinem geschwungenen Giebel und der mit Masken geschmückten Vorderfront und das zeremonielle Versammlungshaus auf Palau, Mikronesien, mit seinen bunten Frontbemalungen waren die Vorbilder für viele amerikanische Tiki-Tempel. Als moderne Primitive der Mittelklasse trafen die Jetsons auf die Feuersteins, parkten ihre Shuttle-Maschinen vor diesen Raumschiffen vom Planet Tiki und überschritten nur allzu gern die Grenze zu einer anderen Dimension, einer anderen Welt, um für eine

gewisse Zeit zu Mitgliedern des Tiki-Stammes zu werden.

A-Formen waren einfach zu bauen, und so wurden herkömmliche Bauten wie Wisconsin-Blockhütten oder klassische Geschäftshäuser in heidnische Paläste umgestaltet, indem man sie um eine spitz zulaufende Eingangshalle erweiterte. Dinarestaurants modernisierten ihr Interieur und übernahmen den Hüttenlook, um von der polynesischen Welle zu profitieren. Doch was spielte sich hinter dem großen A ab? Um die Schwelle zu einer anderen Realität zu symbolisieren, musste häufig eine Brücke überquert werden, die über einen Fluss führte; dieser wurde von einem Wasserfall gespeist, der über einen Lava-Felsen herabfiel. Das Element des Feuers wurde mit ausgetriebenen Tiki-Fackeln ins Spiel gebracht, die manchmal auch als Leuchtfeuer die Spitzen der Giebel zierten, und auch drinnen gab es Wasserfälle, die für ein Plätschern im Hintergrund sorgten. Imponierende Tikis flankierten den Eingang, glotzten zwischen dem Dschungel-Blattwerk hervor und dienten als Pfosten oder hatten andere architektonische Zwecke.

Im Inneren befand sich eine Erlebniswelt, die alle Sinne ansprach. Die verschiedenen Räume trugen malerische Namen wie „Schwarzes Loch von Kalkutta" oder „Salon der sieben Freuden" und waren vom Boden bis zur Decke mit exotischen Hölzern, Bambus, Rattan, Tapa-Stoffen und anderen organischen Materialien ausgekleidet. Primitive Waffen und Masken schmückten die Wände und unter der Decke hingen Beachcomber-Lampen und ähnliches Strandgut. Wandbilder vom Inselleben und dreidimensionale Dioramen verstärkten darüber hinaus die Illusion, sich in einem fernen Teil der Welt zu befinden.

Ein weiteres wichtiges Material war die menschliche Haut: Viele Etablissements rühmten sich ihrer spärlich bekleideten exotischen Kellnerinnen; sie waren die lebendigen Gegenstücke zu den Akten in schwarzem Samt, die ebenfalls zum üblichen Dekor von Tiki-Lokalen gehörten. Für die Krieger im weißen Kragen bedeutete diese Fleischbeschau eine besondere Attraktion, die durch die polynesischen Varieteevorführungen zum üblichen Unterhaltungsprogramm in vielen Südsee-Nachtclubs gehörten. Dass die samoanischen Feuertänzer oder die tahitischen Hula-Mädchen häufig aus Südamerika oder Asien stammten, war dabei nicht wichtig. Die Kostüme und die Musik, die exotischen Materialien, die tropische Ausstattung und die starken Drinks – das alles ergab ein wirksames Gemisch, um alle

kleinlichen Bedenken, ob dies nun authentisch war oder nicht, in Luft aufzulösen; stattdessen durfte sich der Tiki-Nachtschwärmer ganz dem unwirklichen Zauber des städtischen polynesischen Paradieses hingeben.

DON THE BEACHCOMBER – AHNHERR DES POLYNESISCHEN POP

Hollywood 1934: Amerikas „nobles Experiment" mit der Prohibition war gerade beendet worden. Hochprozentiges war gefragt, und ein aus New Orleans zugezogener Gastronom namens Ernest Beaumont-Gantt beschloss, mit Rum ein Experiment zu wagen. Vielleicht war es die Vergangenheit seiner Heimatstadt als Piratennest, vielleicht auch die Tatsache, dass sein Vater, Hotelier in New Orleans, ihn mit auf Reisen nach Jamaika genommen hatte – wie auch immer: Ernest kam auf die Idee, eine kleine Bar am McCadden Place in Hollywood zu eröffnen, die er mit ein paar künstlichen Palmen schmückte und *Don the Beachcomber* nannte. Hier mixte er das flüssige Gold wie ein Alchimist auf der Suche nach dem Stein der Weisen und kreierte dabei hochprozentige Cocktails, mit denen seine Gäste eine Zeit lang an ferne Küsten entfliehen konnten, während draußen das Großstadtleben vorbeirauschte. Ernest identifizierte sich so sehr mit der Figur des Beachcomber, des „Strand-Streichers", dass er seinen Namen offiziell in Don Beach änderte. Seine besonderen Fähigkeiten als Barkeeper zogen schon bald die nach Alkohol und exotischer Atmosphäre lechzende Filmwelt an, und 1937 baute er seine Bar zu einem Südsee-Refugium aus, das zum Vorbild für viele weitere Gastronomen werden sollte: Don gestaltete sein polynesisches Paradies wie eine Insel im Stadtozean, als Zufluchtsort vor der brodelnden Großstadt.

Die Grundausstattung bestand aus exotischen Materialien wie Bambus, Lahaula-Matten und importierten Hölzern. Tropische Pflanzen, frische Blumengirlanden und Gebinde aus Bananen und Kokosnüssen sorgten für die Dschungel-Atmosphäre, während Waffen von Eingeborenen und andere ozeanische Artefakte eine Stimmung primitiver Zivilisationen heraufbeschworen. Strandgut und Krimskrams aus allen Ecken und Enden der Welt hing von der Decke und verstärkte die Illusion, dass man irgendwo in einem Hafen der Freuden gelandet sei. Ein regelmäßig wiederkehrender künstlicher Regenschauer erweckte den Eindruck, dass man gerade einem tropischen Wolkenbruch entgangen sei, während die sanften Töne der ununterbrochen laufenden Hintergrundmusik die Gäste in ihre exotischen Träumereien einlullte. Das Ganze wurde durch Dons hochwirksame Cocktail Kreationen verstärkt, die bisweilen in angehöhlten Ananasfrüchten serviert wurden. Doch was Don Beach an Showtalent und Fantasie besaß, fehlte ihm an Geschäftstüchtigkeit. Um diesen Part kümmerte sich seine Frau Cora Irene „Sunny" Sund. Die geschäftliche Teilhaberschaft mündete 1937 in der Ehe, die aber schon drei Jahre später geschieden wurde. Geschäftlich hielt Sunny die Zügel fest im Griff, so fest, dass Don, als er von seiner Verpflichtung im Kriegsdienst als Oberst der Luftwaffe aus dem Zweiten Weltkriegs zurückkehrte, feststellen musste, dass sie ihn aus seinem eigenen Lokal ausgebootet hatte. Sunny hatte 1940 die Eröffnung des ersten Franchise-Betriebs in Chicago eingeleitet und das Unternehmen war jetzt fest in ihrer Hand; sie brauchte Don nicht mehr, nur noch seinen Namen.

Da Don aber von jeher eher ein Ideengeber denn ein Manager gewesen war, erklärte er sich einverstanden, dem Don the Beachcomber in beratender Funktion zur Seite zu stehen, gleichzeitig aber steckte er all seine kreativen Energien in sein Traumprojekt: ein eigenes Lokal auf Hawaii.

Don hatte aber auch einen Prototyp geschaffen: den urbanen Beachcomber, eine Person irgendwo zwischen weit gereistem Connaisseur, Strand-Beatnik und Jachthafen-Playboy. In der Hochzeit des polynesischen Pop kamen andere Beachcomber zum Vorschein, der bemerkenswerteste unter ihnen Ely Hedley, der auch als der „Original-Beachcomber" bekannt war.

Ehemals ein erfolgloser Lebensmittelhändler in Oklahoma, war er dem Ruf des Pazifischen Ozeans gefolgt und mit seiner Familie nach Whites Point, einer kleinen Bucht in der Nähe von San Pedro bei Los Angeles, gezogen. Dort baute er mit seiner Frau und seinen vier Töchtern ein Haus aus Treibholz und begann seine florierenden Handel mit Lampen und Möbeln, die sie aus dem Treibgut und Fundsachen herstellten, der ihnen vors Haus gespült wurde. Ely wurde so bekannt für seinen Stil, „Beachcomber modern" genannt, dass er Aufträge zur Einrichtung von Tiki-Tempeln wie Trader Dick's und Harvey's in Nevada bekam. Als das Tiki-Fieber ausbrach, fing er an, Tikis zu schnitzen, und eröffnete seinen Island Trade Store zuerst in Huntington Beach und dann im Adventureland in Disneyland. Nachdem Ely Hedley den Tiki-Stil entscheidend mitgeprägt hatte, zog er sich in die Islander-Apartments in Santa Ana zurück, die er selbst eingerichtet hatte.

In der Zwischenzeit war Don the Beachcomber zu einem kommerziellen Markenzeichen geworden und das Geschäft war schon zweimal in andere Hände übergegangen, um schließlich im Besitz der Getty-Corporation zu landen. Die Logo-Figur ähnelte nun nicht mehr dem leibhaftigen Don, sondern war modernisiert worden und sah wie irgendein x-beliebiger, freundlicher Lebenskünstler aus. Das Franchise-Unternehmen war auf 16 Lokale angewachsen, von denen einige, etwa das in Dallas und in Marina Del Rey, wie braune Ufos aussahen. Andere Polynesienbegeisterte überall in den Staaten hatten sich vom Beachcomber-Vorbild beeinflussen lassen, aber keiner kam an Dons Flair heran. Wenige Jahre nach Dons Tod im Jahre 1987 wurden auch die Überreste der Restaurantkette, die seinen Namen trug, aber schon lange ohne sein „Mana" existiert hatte, geschlossen. Sein prägender Einfluss auf das Phänomen des polynesischen Pop jedoch bleibt unvergessen.

TRADER VIC – DER BOTSCHAFTER DES GUTEN GESCHMACKS

Die Amerikanisierung von Tiki als einem Freizeitgott war ein allmählicher Prozess. Einer seiner wichtigsten Propheten war ein Mann namens Victor Bergeron, besser bekannt als Trader Vic. Zwar stellte er die Gottheit nicht ins Zentrum seiner Religion – er benutzte vielmehr seine eigenen mythologischen Figuren, das „kleine Volk" aus den polynesischen Legenden –, doch seit Beginn der 50er Jahre war Tiki immer um ihn. Und der Trader war eine jener überlebensgroßen Figuren, ein Original, Angehöriger einer aussterbenden Spezies von einzigartigen Charakteren, wie man sie heute im öffentlichen Leben nicht mehr findet.

Er war Patriarch, Gentleman und Chauvinist zugleich; ein erfolgreicher Gastronom und Genussmensch, der eine ganze Generation von kultivierten Wilden dazu anregte, der Zivilisation den Rücken zu kehren, und sich in Bars und Restaurants, in Gärten, Hinterhöfen und auf Bowlingbahnen ein eigenes Polynesien zu schaffen. Er erhob das Essen und Trinken nach Südseeart zu einer Kunst – „chow and grog", wie er es in seiner rauen Art zu nennen pflegte. Mehr noch als Don the Beachcomber, der angeblich auf den Namen „Rumaki" für seine Vorspeisenkreation gekommen ist, indem er mit seinem Finger in die Seiten eines Lexikons mit den Cook-Inseln stach, war Trader Vic ein richtiger kulinarischer Erneuerer. Nach seinem Erfolg mit dem „Nouveau Polynesian"-Stil gehörte er zu den ersten, die die mexikanische Küche in Amerika populär machten.

Es begann alles in einem Lokal namens Hinky Dinks in Oakland auf der anderen Seite der Bucht von San Francisco. Dies war Vics erster eigener Laden, eine Holzhütte, die er 1934 mit seinen letzten 500 Dollar errichtet hatte. In der Geschichte des polynesischen Pop gab es bestimmte „Energiezentren" wie das Beachcomber in Hollywood, das Luau in Beverly Hills, das Lanai in San Mateo oder das Bali Ha'i in San Diego, die das Mana der Tiki-Kultur ausstrahlten. Hinki Dinks, das bald Trader Vic's heißen sollte, gehörte dazu. Victor Bergeron war ein ehrgeiziger Mann mit einer Vorliebe für fantasievolle Cocktails, und genau danach hatten die Leute Sehnsucht, nachdem die Prohibition endlich aufgehoben war. Er ging auf eine „Forschungsreise" nach Kuba und Louisiana und experimentierte an Ort und Stelle mit den Top-Barkeepern. Aber ein Besuch in Los Angeles hatte den entscheidenden Einfluss. In seiner Biografie verrät er: „Wir fuhren zu einem Lokal namens South Seas, das es heute nicht mehr gibt, und besuchten auch das Don the Beachcomber in Hollywood. Ich habe sogar ein paar Flaschen im Don the Beachcomber gekauft. Als ich wieder in Oakland war und meiner Frau erzählte, was ich gesehen hatte, waren wir uns einig, den Namen unseres Restaurants zu ändern und auch die gesamte Einrichtung. Wir fanden beide, dass Hinky Dinks ein blöder Name war und das Lokal nach jemandem benannt werden sollte, über den wir etwas zu erzählen hatten. Meine Frau schlug Trader Vic's vor, weil ich ständig mit irgendjemandem Geschäfte machte. So war es, ich wurde also Trader Vic." Daraufhin bekam das Holzbein, das die Folge einer Tuberkuloseerkrankung in seiner Kindheit war (und das schon manchmal dazu gedient hatte, seine Gäste zu unterhalten, indem er völlig überraschend einen Eispickel hineinstach), eine neue Geschichte: Er habe es der Begegnung mit einem Hai zu verdanken – eines der vielen Märchen, die auf Vics neue Rolle zugeschnitten waren.

Das freimütige Geständnis des Ursprungs des Trader Vic betreffend kam von einem Mann, der nicht nur genauso viel wie sein Kollege und Vorgänger erreicht, sondern ihn sogar übertrumpft hatte. Vic musste nie verheimlichen, wo seine Ursprünge lagen, denn er hatte nie die Leitung seines Unternehmens verloren, wie es Don passiert war, und als der polynesische Trend in den 50er Jahren richtig los ging, war er in der Lage, ihn voll zu nutzen. Nachdem er 1949 seine erste Filiale in Seattle gegründet hatte, die er The Outrigger nannte, folgten Lokale in San Francisco (1951), Denver (1954), Beverly Hills (1955), Chicago (1957), New York und Havanna (1958) und Portland (1959); später in Boston, Houston, Dallas, Detroit, Atlanta, Kansas City, St. Louis, St.

Petersburg, Washington, Vancouver, Scottsdale, London, München und in vielen anderen Städten im Ausland.

Vic weitete seinen Einfluss noch weiter aus, indem er Cocktail- und Rezeptbücher veröffentlichte, in denen er bevorzugt Produkte aus seiner neuen „Trader Vic's Food Products Company" verwendete. In diesen Veröffentlichungen breitete er seine Ansichten über gesellige Zusammenkünfte und Essgewohnheiten der Mittelklasse aus, und zwar in seinem charakteristischen Trader Vic-Tonfall, der sich deutlich von der blumigen Prosa unterschied, die er in seinen Speisekarten verwendete: „Es gibt ein paar Sachen, die mir besonders sauer aufstoßen, wenn ich sehe, was da zusammengekocht wird, wenn man mal bei jemandem eingeladen wird, wo's ein bisschen was zu Essen und zu Trinken geben soll. Ich bin dafür, dass die durchschnittliche amerikanische Gastgeberin einen leichten Tritt in den kulinarischen Hinterteil vertragen kann, legen wir also los. Die Leckerbissen, die üblicherweise auf Cocktailpartys serviert werden, bringen mich ganz einfach um. Nachdem ich nun viele Jahre lang Hunderte von Silbertabletts und ihren Inhalt angeguckt habe, bin ich zu dem Schluss gekommen, dass irgendjemand einen jährlichen Pulitzerpreis für das absolut tödlichste Hors d'œuvre ausgeschrieben hat." Der Trader spielte ein grantiges Rauhbein, und die Leute liebten ihn dafür.

Als Hawaii Amerikas Ferientraumziel Nummer eins wurde, engagierte man Vic, um als Ernährungsberater für die United Airlines und die Hotels der Matson-Reederei zu fungieren, die die beiden wichtigsten Reiseunternehmen zwischen den Inseln und den USA waren. Schon früher, um 1940, war er eine Partnerschaft eingegangen, um ein Lokal in Honolulu zu eröffnen, doch aufgrund von Meinungsverschiedenheiten zog er sich daraus zurück und überließ der anderen Seite das Recht, seinen Namen auf den Inseln zu benutzen. Die Tatsache, dass ein ursprünglich aus Kalifornien stammendes Trader Vic's auf Hawaii eröffnet wurde, dem später auch ein Don the Beachcomber, Stephen Cranes Kon-Tiki und Christian's Hut folgten, stützt die Behauptung, der polynesische Pop sei tatsächlich eine Facette der amerikanischen Popkultur und nach Hawaii importiert worden, um die Erwartungen der Touristen zu erfüllen.

Die Ausweitung des Trader-Imperiums wurde durch die Zusammenarbeit mit finanzstarken größeren Hotelketten ermöglicht. Sie hatten die finanziellen Mittel, so raffinierte Bauten hinzustellen, wie ein Tiki-Lokal der Extraklasse es erforderte,

und Trader Vic's war Extraklasse. Andere Südseekneipen, die häufig seinen Spitznamen kopierten, waren eher für das gemeine Fußvolk gedacht, während Vic's der Offiziersclub war. Aber nicht etwa, weil Vic ein Snob war, sondern weil er Geld damit verdienen wollte. Doch letztlich war dies einer der Gründe für den Untergang der Kette, denn als die Oberschichtenklientel, die diese Genusstempel aufzusuchen pflegte, ausstarb, suchte die jüngere Generation nach erschwinglicheren und weniger gekünstelten Lokalitäten.

Bedauerlicherweise sind in den 90er Jahren noch die Filialen in Seattle, Washington, Vancouver, Portland und sogar in San Francisco geschlossen worden. Aber in Übersee hält sich Trader Vic's gut und ist die einzige Kette mit Tiki-Lokalen, die bis heute überlebt hat. Trotz der misslungenen Renovierungen in den 80er Jahren, bei denen die charakteristischen Vogelkäfiglampen und andere traditionelle Einrichtungsstücke als „Staubfänger" hinausgeworfen wurden, gibt es immer noch Trader Vic's in Chicago und München, die als seltene Beispiele für den Tiki-Stil erhalten geblieben sind.

STEPHEN CRANE – DER MANN, DER DIE FRAUEN LIEBTE

In polynesischen Legenden von der Insel Mangareva und den Marquesa-Inseln wird Tiki, der erste Mann, als Gauner und Frauenheld dargestellt. Schließlich war es er, der die erste Frau aus Lehm schuf und sogleich daranging, alle Kinder dieser Welt mit ihr zu machen. Daher scheint es nur recht und billig, dass der nächste, der die Tiki-Fackel übernahm, ein Mann war, der für seine Gesellichkeit bekannt war und Frauen im Nu eroberte. Er war ein erfolgloser B-Picture-Schauspieler („Cry of the Werewolf"), und sein einziger Anspruch auf Ruhm gründete darin, mit Lana Turner verheiratet gewesen zu sein. Die Ehe hielt nur fünf Monate, aber sie hatten eine gemeinsame Tochter, Cheryl, die später als Teenager in die Schlagzeilen geriet, weil sie Lanas Mafioso-Liebhaber Johnny Stompanato erstochen hatte (was damit zu tun hatte, dass sie zuvor schon von einem anderen Verehrer ihrer Mutter, dem Film-Tarzan Lex Barker, vergewaltigt worden war). Stephen aber blieb mit Lana befreundet, während er daranging, weitere Filmstars zu verführen. Der Besitzer von Ciro's, Hollywoods berühmtestem Ausgehlokal in den 40er Jahren, bemerkte staunend, nachdem er Steve an den irgendwie folgenden Abenden mit Ava Gardner, Rita Hayworth und Lana Turner gesehen hatte: „Mit den drei absoluten Königinnen der Stadt! Ich hab noch nie jemanden kennen-

gelernt, der das geschafft hat."

Glücklicherweise konzentrierte Stephen Crane seine Energie schon bald auf sein anderes Talent, Restaurants zu organisieren und zu unterhalten. 1953 eröffnete er das Restaurant Luau in Beverly Hills am 421 Rodeo Drive. Dort war vorher das Südseelokal The Tropic beheimatet gewesen, und Stephen baute die thematische Ausrichtung des Lokals weiter aus, wobei er im Sinn hatte, die Klientel aus der „Filmkolonie" anzuziehen. Er tat dies auf seine Weise, wie sich seine Tochter Cheryl in ihrer Biografie „Detour – A Hollywood Story" erinnert: „Er überlegte sich, dass Männer besonders gern in solche Lokale gingen, die auch für Frauen attraktiv waren, und darum wollte er den Ort so verführerisch machen wie eine Honigfalle … Das Herzstück von Daddys Honigfalle war eine wenig bekannte und nie hinausposaunte Regel, dass er männlich ausgewählten und sehr teuren Callgirls erlaubte, sich diskret an der Bar aufzuhalten. Es waren häufig erfolglose Starlets, aufregend und geschmackvoll gekleidet, die den Männern anzogen, für weibliche Gäste jedoch kein Störfaktor waren, da diese nur selten erkannten, um wen es sich dabei wirklich handelte."

Um das Prinzip „Die Schöne und das Biest" voll zum Tragen kommen zu lassen, bevölkerte Crane sein Paradies mit Tikis und stellte sie in seiner Speisekarte vor: „Von besonderem Interesse sind die Tikis, die großen und wunderbar ungraziösen Holzfiguren, die Sie um sich haben. Ein Tiki ist ein heidnischer Gott, ein Götze. Obwohl heute die meisten Bewohner der Südseeinseln Christen sind, bringen sie den Göttern ihrer Vorfahren immer noch Respekt und Verehrung entgegen, und hier bei uns im Luau haben wir Tikis u. a. als Regengott, Sonnengott und Kriegsgott. Der Tiki mit dem besonders großen Mund ist der Gott des Trinkens, der Großmäulige. Der Tiki mit dem größten Bauch ist unser Lieblingsgott, vielleicht weil er der Gott des guten Essens ist." Dieser humorvolle und naive Umgang mit der erloschenen Religion eines anderen Volkes sollte fortan für den Tiki-Stil charakteristisch sein. Zum ersten Mal wurde ein Tiki, der den beiden holzgeschnitzten Eingangsposten ähnlich sah, als Sinnbild auf der Speisekarte, den Streichhölzern und Postkarten sowie für den Fuß einer Keramiklampe und als Salz- und Pfefferstreuer verwendet.

Für die übrige Einrichtung hatte Stephen kräftig Anleihen beim Beachcomber und Trader Vic genommen. Artdirector Florian Gabriel erinnert sich, dass Stephen Crane and Associates für seinen Job von ihm erwarteten, ins Trader Vic's im Beverly Hilton (das sich einst rühmen konnte, fünf Tikis von 4,5 Meter Höhe vor dem Lokal stehen zu haben) zu gehen um eine Ecke des Restaurants zu skizzieren, was ihm auch gelang. Er bildete gemeinsam mit George Nakashima, der zuvor für Welton Becket, den Architekten des *Beverly Hilton*, gearbeitet hatte ein Einrichtungsteam. Sie wirkten auch daran mit, die Filialen aufzubauen, die Stephen Crane am Ende der 50er Jahre in anderen amerikanischen Städten errichtete.

Die Sheraton Corporation, die unbedingt mit dem *Hilton* gleichziehen wollte, bat Crane gebeten ein Lokal wie sein *Luau* in ihrem Hotel in Montreal einzurichten; es wurde 1958 unter dem Namen *Kon-Tiki* eröffnet und präsentierte sich den begeisterten Publikum mit „von den Maoris handgeschnitzten Wandtäfelungen mit speziellen Mustern, um böse Geister fernzuhalten, mit Speeren aus Neuguinea, dem Fledermausflügel-Spitzen von den Jägern in Gift getaucht wurden, und einem Opferaltar". In den nächsten Jahren folgten dann Portland (mit drei Wasserfällen!), Chicago, Dallas, Cleveland und Honolulu. Das *Kon-Tiki Ports* in Chicago und das *Ports of Call* in Dallas entwickelten das Konzept des Westentaschen-Abenteurers weiter und gestalteten jeden Speisesaal nach einem anderen Motto: Papeete, Singapur, Macao und Saigon. Ihre Geschichten waren reinste polynesische Pop-Poesie: „*Papeete* – einer von vier exotischen Aufenthaltsräumen im Ports o' Call Restaurant im Penthouse des Southland Center, Dallas, Texas. Für dieses tropische Lokal ist die Natur domestiziert worden. Ein Wasserfall plätschert zu ihrem Vergnügen, während einheimische Wildtiere bewegungslos verharren, damit sie sich so richtig wohlfühlen. Doch Speere und Felle erinnern den Gast daran, dass auch das einfache Leben seine aufregenden Seiten hat."

Aber die Kluft, die sich schon bald zwischen der Tiki-Generation und ihren gegen den Vietnamkrieg protestierenden Kindern auftat, ist wohl am besten in der Beschreibung des Saigon-Raums zum Ausdruck gebracht: „Orientalische Pracht und Opulenz bestimmen diesen Hafen der Sinnenfreuden. Seine glücklichen Bewohner sind umgeben von echtem Blattgold, seltener Seide, feinstem Kristall und intro verbotenen Tempelschnitzereien". Was 1960 noch als poetische Phantasie erlaubt war, hatte sich 1968 in schmerzlichen Sarkasmus verwandelt. Ende der 70er Jahre bot ein iranisches Konsortium Stephen Crane 4,1 Millionen Dollar für das *Luau*. 1979 wurde es bis auf die Grundfesten niedergerissen, ein deutliches Signal für das Ende der Tiki-Ära.

DANNY BALSZ – DER VERLORENE SOHN

Die Gestalt des Danny Balsz lässt sich nicht nahtlos in die Reihe der Ahnherren des polynesischen Pop einordnen. Weder begründete er eine Restaurantkette, noch glänzte er mit kulinarischen oder alkoholischen Neuerungen. Er befasste sich weniger mit Qualität denn mit Quantität. Für Danny Balsz lautete die Devise „Größer ist besser", und somit baute er den größten Vulkan auf dem ausgedehntesten polynesischen Luau-Gelände des Landes. Hier wurde jede Nacht eine Tiki-Jungfrau als Opfer in seinen gefräßigen Schlund geworfen, während tahitische Tänzerinnen, deren Kostüme eher aus Las Vegas als von den Südseeinseln zu stammen schienen, sich nach den Rhythmen verschiedener Bands wiegten. Als er herausfand, dass die Hawaiianer angeblich daran glaubten, dass das Glück von der Anzahl der Tikis abhänge, die man in seinem Hause habe, umgab er sich mit Holzfiguren aller Größen und Formen und nannte den Ort *The Tikis*. Mehr Götter, mehr Tänzer, mehr Essen und Trinken für mehr als 3000 Gäste pro Nacht. Das war Tiki für die Massen, und Danny war Mr. Tiki!

The Tikis stellt den Höhepunkt der gesamten Tiki-Ära dar, die sich noch einmal mit einer nie da gewesenen Grandiosität und Dekadenz präsentierte, bevor sie aus dem kulturellen Leben verschwand und in Vergessenheit geriet. Als ich über die Ruinen dieses vergessenen Disneylands der Götter stolperte, wusste ich, dass seine Geschichte eines Tages erzählt werden müsste. Vor mir lag der verlorene Planet der Tikis, der Elefantenfriedhof einer erloschenen Spezies. Was hatte zum Niedergang dieser einst so großartigen Zivilisation geführt?

Danny Balsz war der Sohn eines Nachtclubbesitzers aus der Grenzstadt Mexicale, im Kopf viele Erinnerungen an einen zwielichtigen Glanz. Zehn Jahre lang arbeitete er als Metzger in einem Schlachthaus, bis er beschloss, in die Landschaftsgärtnerei zu wechseln; dort spezialisierte er sich auf Wasserfälle. 1958 holte Danny Pflanzmaterial aus einer japanischen Baumschule in Monterey Park, einem ländlichen Vorort von Los Angeles, der eingeklemmt zwischen vier Schnellstraßen lag. Als er an einer benachbarten Hühnerfarm hielt, traf er die Besitzerin Doris Samson. Vier Monate später waren sie verheiratet. Während er Doris bei der Hühnerhaltung half, baute er sein Können in der Landschaftsgestaltung aus und verwandelte den halben Hektar Grundbesitz in einen tropischen Garten. 1960 fragten zwei College-Studenten bei Danny an, ob sie auf seinem

Grund eine Luau-Party veranstalten dürften. Zu jener Zeit schoossen Luau-Anlagen, die man für Partys mieten konnte, in Südkalifornien wie Pilze aus dem Boden. Danny und Doris beschlossen, ihre sämtlichen Hühner zu schlachten und im polynesischen Party-Geschäft ihr Glück zu versuchen. Sie kamen genau zur richtigen Zeit, ihre Anlage wuchs und gedieh, und Jahr für Jahr goss und formte Danny mehr Beton zu Lava-Tunneln, Tropfsteinhöhlen und Wasserfälle und schuf eigenhändig sein persönliches Xanadu.

In den 60er Jahren wurde seine Kundschaft, die vor allem aus der Arbeiterklasse stammte, in Bussen von den Flugzeugfabriken und Speditionsunternehmen herbeigekarrt. Die nötigen Vorräte, zum Beispiel 50 000 hawaiische Blütenkränze aus der Plastikblumenfabrik in Hughestown, Pennsylvania, und tonnenweise Ananas wurden bar bezahlt, und wenn noch Geld übrig war, kaufte Danny noch mehr Tikis. „Ich kann dir sagen, ich hatte alles: Geld, Autos, Ringe!" erinnert sich Danny. Aber er wollte mehr. Dannys Glückssträhne ging zu Ende, als er die Ursünde beging: Er verliebte sich in Leilani, eine mormonische hawaiische Tänzerin in *The Tikis*. Die Verbindung zwischen dem Haole und der Wahine wurde von den Göttern nicht gutgeheißen, und noch viel weniger von Dannys Frau und seinen Kindern, die das Rückgrat seines Familienunternehmens gewesen waren. Unter dem Druck von Nachbarn, die ohnehin seit langem die Nase voll hatten, wiederrief der Stadtrat seine Lizenz für das Unterhaltungsgeschäft. Der polynesische Affenzirkus war vorüber, so schien es. Aber Danny Balsz war ein ehrgeiziger Mann. Er packte seine Tikis ein und baute ihnen in Lake Elsinore, noch weiter südlich von Los Angeles gelegen, eine neue Heimat. Dort arbeitete er jahrelang am Aufbau eines völlig neuen Lavalandes. Geduldig wachten seine Tikis über seine Arbeit und warteten auf die große Neueröffnung. Aber die Zeiten hatten sich geändert, und der große Tag kam nie. „Das Licht, das doppelt so hell brennt, brennt halb so lang, und du hast doch so hell, so leuchtend hell gebrannt. Du bist der verlorene Sohn! – Aber ich habe zweifelhafte Dinge getan ... Auch großartige Dinge, du hast deine Zeit in vollen Zügen genossen ..." (aus Ridley Scotts „Bladerunner")

KON-TIKI, AKU AKU UND THOR

„Die ungelösten Rätsel der Südsee hatten mich in ihren Bann gezogen. Es muss eine rationale Lösung dafür geben, und ich setzte mir zum Ziel, die Sagengestalt Tiki zu identifizieren." So sprach ein junger norwegischer Zoologe namens Thor Heyerdahl im Jahre 1937, während er auf Fatu Hiva, einer zur Marquesa-Gruppe gehörenden Insel im zentralen Pazifik, ums Überleben kämpfte. Heyerdahl führte dort mit seiner Frau eine Art „Hippie-Leben". Thor und Liv hatten beschlossen, die Zivilisation hinter sich zu lassen und „zurückzukehren zur Natur". Wie Primitive lebten sie auf ihrer Insel, deren Fauna sie für die Universität Oslo untersuchten. Doch als Thor den alten Tei Tetua, den letzten Eingeborenen, der ein „Long Pig" (einen Menschen) gekostet hatte, am abendlichen Feuer ein altes Volksmärchen erzählen hörte, änderte sich alles. „Tiki war Gott und Häuptling zugleich. Tiki war es, der unsere Vorväter auf die Inseln gebracht hat, auf denen wir heute leben. Früher lebten wir in einem großen Land, weit hinter dem Meer."

Thor kam auf die Idee, seinen Forschungsgegenstand von Schnecken und riesigen giftigen Tausendfüßlern auf den Ursprung der polynesischen Rasse zu verlagern. Ihm war die Ähnlichkeit der marquesischen Stein-Tikis und Felszeichnungen (Petroglyphen) mit den Götzenbildern der Inkas in Peru aufgefallen, und während der nächsten zehn Jahre arbeitete er an seiner Theorie, dass der Prä-Inka-Hohe Priester und Sonnengott Kon-Tici Viracocha, der von einem kriegerischen Häuptling gezwungen worden war, aus Peru zu fliehen, identisch mit dem polynesischen Gott und Stammesvater Tiki war. Da Thor nur auf erbitterten Widerstand seitens der Archäologen, Ethnologen, Linguisten und Soziologen stieß, und gerade, um seine Theorie in der Praxis zu beweisen. Er baute ein präkolumbianisches Floss aus Balsaholz, für das er nicht eine einzige Eisenstift, Nagel oder Draht verwendete, nannte es „Kon-Tiki" und ließ sich und seine fünf Mann Besatzung auf dem Humboldtstrom von Peru nach Polynesien treiben.

Nach nur drei Monaten auf hoher See erreichte das Floß leicht versehrt die polynesischen Küstengewässer. Der Reisebericht erschien 1948 unter dem Titel „Die Kon-Tiki-Expedition" zuerst in Norwegen und erhielt ziemlich schlechte Besprechungen: Das ganze Unternehmen sei damit vergleichbar, „in einem Fass die Niagarafälle hinunterzufahren". Doch das große Interesse des breiten Publikum blieb von diesen Kritiken unberührt. Als das Buch 1950 in England und Amerika veröffentlicht wurde, stellte sich schnell heraus, dass die Verleger einen Bestseller im Programm hatten. Schließlich wurde „Kon-Tiki" in sechzig Sprachen übersetzt, nur die Bibel hatte weltweit größere Verbreitung gefunden. Die Verfilmung der Rei-

se erlitt ein ähnliches Schicksal: Von amerikanischen Verleihern zunächst wegen technischer Schwächen abgelehnt, erhielt der Film 1951 dennoch den Oscar als bester Dokumentarfilm, und Millionen von Menschen haben ihn gesehen. Die Welt begann gerade, sich vom Trauma des Zweiten Weltkrieges zu erholen und sehnte sich nach friedfertigen Abenteuern.

Die beispiellose weltweite Kon-Tiki-Begeisterung heizte das Interesse der Amerikaner an der polynesischen Kultur weiter an. Obwohl „Tiki-Stil" in den 50er und 60er Jahren kein gängiger Begriff war, sprach man doch gemeinhin vom „Kon-Tiki-Stil" wenn man die polynesischen Architektur meinte. Thor und Tiki, der nordische Gott des Donners und der polynesische Gott der Sonne, hatten sich zum Pophelden zu werden. Heyerdahls Buch „Aku Aku" von 1955 über seine Osterinsel-Expedition erwies sich als ebenso einflussreich für den polynesischen Pop. Der Buchumschlag wurde zu einer so populären Ikone, dass die riesigen Steinstatuen, die eigentlich „Moai" heißen, als „Aku Aku-Köpfe" oder eben als „Aku-Tikis" bekannt wurden, und zu einem weit verbreiteten Motiv im amerikanischen Tiki-Kult wurden.

JAMES MICHENER UND BALI HA'I

„Bali Hai wird dich vielleicht rufen, Tag und Nacht.
Mit deinem Herzen wirst du es hören, komm her, komm her.
Bali Hai säuselt im Wind, rauscht im Meer, Ich bin hier, deine eigene geheime Insel, komm her, komm her.
Deine geheimsten Wünsche, deine geheimsten Träume,
Umspielen hier die Gipfel und glitzern dort in Flüsschen.
Wenn du suchst, wirst du mich finden, wo Himmel und Meer sich treffen
Ich bin hier, deine geheime Insel, komm her, komm her."
(aus Rodgers & Hammerstein's „South Pacific")

Thor Heyerdahl war nicht der einzige Bestseller-Autor, der einen Beitrag zum polynesischen Pop leistete. Während des Zweiten Weltkriegs kam eine ganze Generation amerikanischer Wehrpflichtiger in direkten Kontakt mit der Kultur der Pazifik-Inseln, darunter auch James Michener. Sein fiktionaler Bericht über ihre schrecklichen Erlebnisse („Tales of the South Pacific", dt. „Im Korallenmeer") erhielt 1948 den Pulitzerpreis und wurde ein riesiger Publikumserfolg. Ein Broadway-Musical und ein Breitwandfilm romantisierten die tatsächliche Härte und Unerbittlichkeit des Krieges so erfolgreich, dass ein neuer Begriff für das „exotische Paradies" erfunden

wurde: das fiktive „Bali Ha'i", die Insel der Frauen. Es wurde das neue Shangri-La, die Trauminsel schlechthin.

Dort erlebte die Hauptfigur des Romans, Leutnant Cable, die jahrhundertealte Männerfantasie einer zwanglosen Liebe zu einer jungen exotischen Schönheit. Dem Protagonisten wird das Privileg zugestanden, die Insel, „ein Juwel im weiten Ozean", zu besuchen, auf der „die Franzosen mit gallischem Weitblick und Kennerschaft in diesen Dingen, alle jungen Frauen von den umliegenden Inseln untergebracht hatten. Jedes Mädchen, egal welcher Hautfarbe und ob hübsch oder hässlich, das sonst von amerikanischen Soldaten vergewaltigt worden wäre, wurde auf Bali Ha'i versteckt." (Michener)

Als Leutnant Cables Boot dort vor Anker geht, wird er wohl von jedem männlichen Leser in den 50er Jahren beneidet: „Zum ersten Mal in seinem Leben hatte er so viele Frauen gesehen, ja überhaupt Frauen, die bis zur Hüften hinunter völlig unbekleidet waren … Wie im Dschungel, wie die Früchte des Dschungels schien es hier junge Mädchen in unglaublicher Fülle zu geben." (Michener)

Cable wird schon bald von der eingeborenen Matrone Bloody Mary vor den Heerscharen junger Mädchen gerettet und Mary bringt ihn unverzüglich mit ihrer hübschen, jungfräulichen Tochter Liat zusammen. Im Film betritt unser Held eine romantische Palmenhütte, wo Liat ihn erwartet, eine hinreißende Schönheit, die für die Liebe bereit ist. Es wird kein Wort gesprochen, nur sehnsüchtige Blicke, zitternde Lippen, sie verlieben sich auf der Stelle und die Liebe ist tief. Offenbar sind die Urbilder aus der Südsee doch wahr.

Der Umstand, dass Amerikaner aus allen Lebensbereichen plötzlich aus erster Hand mit einer völlig fremden Kultur bekannt gemacht wurden, hinterließ einen unauslöschlichen Eindruck auf Amerika: „Was mache ich hier? Wie bin ich, Joe Cable aus Philadelphia, ausgerechnet hier gelandet? Dies hier ist Bali Ha'i, und vor einem Jahr hatte ich noch nie davon gehört. Was mache ich hier?" (Michener) Die Soldaten reagierten mit kindlichem Staunen und da sie als Retter von den verhassten Japanern herzlich empfangen worden waren, kehrten sie mit eher heiteren und aufregenden Erinnerungen in die U. S. A. zurück. Die Folge war, dass überall kleine Bali Ha'is aus dem Boden schossen, die nicht nur bei denen beliebt waren, die einmal dort gewesen waren.

Das tatsächliche Bali Ha'i auf der kleinen Insel Mono in der Nähe von Guadalcanal hatte Michener kennen gelernt und obwohl er es als „einen dreckigen, unangenehmen Ort" empfand, machte er sich eine Notiz zu seinem Namen, weil sein „musikalischer Klang" ihm gefiel. Dies bewährte den polynesischen Pop-Mythos von Bali Ha'i nicht davor, schließlich nach Französisch-Polynesien reimportiert zu werden. Im Jahre 1961 beschlossen ein Börsenmakler, ein Rechtsanwalt und ein Sportartikelverkäufer, die offenbar vom Tiki-Fieber erfasst waren, ihr zivilisiertes Leben im Küstenvorort Newport Beach vor Los Angeles hinter sich zu lassen und sich nach Tahiti aufzumachen. Dort eröffneten sie ein Hotel und nannten es selbstverständlich „Bali Ha'i". Die Fiktion hatte über die Wirklichkeit gesiegt, wie so oft im polynesischen Pop.

BAR-KÜNSTLER UND KREATIONEN
von Jeff Berry

Welches Restaurant könnte es sich leisten, Konservenbst auf einem Löffel Hüttenkäse „Ports of Desire" zu nennen? Das Luau konnte – vor allem darum, weil es die besten exotischen Rum-Drinks in ganz Beverly Hills servierte. Solche Drinks waren das Öl im Getriebe der polynesischen Restaurants, sie hielten das Geschäft am Laufen. Sie waren mehr als nur Cocktails. Von Anfang an wurden sie als farbenprächtige Fantasiegebilde angeboten, die ebenso das Auge wie die Zunge erfreuen sollten, und sie wurden mit ausgefallenen Garnierungen und in ebenso ausgefallenen Gefäßen serviert. Sogar das Eis, das sie kühl halten sollte, war in ungewöhnliche Formen gegossen, zum Beispiel als ein geölter Zylinder, in dem der Strohhalm steckte, oder als Iglu, so dass der Drink „in einer Eishöhle schlummernd" am Tisch serviert wurde. Aber genauso gut konnte der Drink rauchend, Flammen sprühend oder mit einer Gardenie verziert, in der eine versteckte Perle auf ihre Entdeckung wartete, beim Gast ankommen.

Das war der Cocktail als Konversationsstück. Wenn man ein polynesisches Restaurant verließ, sprach man nicht über das Essen, sondern über einen „Mystery Drink" oder den „Penang Afridídí" oder „Peles Bucket of Fire". Und der Service begann meistens mit einem Hinweis auf die Karte, auf der die Drinks in poetischen Beschreibungen mit detailbesessenen, bunten Illustrationen dargestellt waren. So nannte The Islander seinen „Mount Kilauea" „eine Eruption feinsten Rum-Imports, gekrönt mit dem heiligen Nektar der Tiki-Götter".

Wie Sie sich wohl denken können, haben diese teuflischen Mischungen nicht immer so gut geschmeckt, wie sie aussahen. Aber die besten tropischen Drinks konnten sehr komplex und nuancenreich sein, zugleich fein und sinnlich, in einer heiklen Balance von süß und sauer, stark und leicht, fruchtig und trocken. Die besten tropischen Drinks wurden im Don the Beachcomber kreiert.

Als Don 1934 seine erste Bar eröffnete, galt Rum als indiskutabel. Alkoholiker hießen „Rummies". Nur Seemänner und Säufer tranken Teufelsrum; die bessere Gesellschaft trank Bourbon und Gin. Warum hat Don also keine Whiskey- und Gin-Drinks kreiert? Weil Rum billiger war! Als die Prohibition beendet wurde, konnte man das Zeug kistenweise für gerade mal siebzig Cents den Liter kaufen. In Dons Fall war Sparsamkeit die Mutter des Gedankens.

Aber Don erfand seine „Rum-Rhapsodien" nicht aus dem Nichts heraus. Nash Aranas, früher für die „Authentizitätskontrolle" in der Beachcomber-Restaurantkette zuständig, verriet 1989, dass Don „eine Zeit lang in Westindien gewesen war, wo ihm die Rum-Idee gekommen war". Wahrscheinlich lernte Don dort den jamaikanischen Planter's Punch und den kubanischen Daiquiri kennen; diese beiden Drinks sind eine einfache Mischung aus Limettensaft, Zucker und Rum – drei Zutaten, die zu den Grundbestandteilen der meisten von Dons Kreationen wurden. Zu den Limetten fügte er Ananas, Papaya und Passionsfrucht hinzu; zum Zucker gab er Anis, Vanille und Mandelextrakt; zum Rum mischte er Schnäpse, parfümierte Brandies ... und noch mehr Rum, sehr viel mehr Rum! Don hatte nämlich entdeckt, dass die Mischung dunkler und heller Rumsorten einen völlig neuen, komplexeren Basisgeschmack erzeugte, der seinen Kompositionen ganz neue Akzente verlieh. „Don konnte den ganzen Tag mit seinen alten Freunden dasitzen und Drinks mixen", erinnert sich Aranas. „Er probierte und probierte und probierte wie ein verrückter Wissenschaftler." Die Kombinationen waren endlos und wurden endlos variiert, und dabei kamen so populäre Kreationen heraus wie seine frühen Erfindungen Vicious Virgin, Shark's Tooth, Cobra's Fang, Dr. Funk und Missionary's Downfall.

Der Legende zufolge soll Dons berühmtester Drink, der Zombie, entstanden sein, als man einem verkaterten Gast, der einen wichtigen geschäftlichen Termin durchstehen hatte, wieder auf die Beine zu helfen versuchte. Als dieser Gast später gefragt wurde, wie der Kur geholfen habe, sagte er: „Ich fühlte mich wie ein lebender Toter – sie hat einen Zombie aus mir gemacht." Doch eine Speisekarte aus dem Beachcomber von 1941 erzählt eine andere Entstehungsgeschichte: „Der Zombie ist nicht durch Zufall entstanden. Er ist das Ergebnis eines langen und teuren Entwick-

lungsprozesses. Für die Experimente, die schließlich zum Zombie führten, wurden dreieinhalb Kisten ausgesuchten Rums verbraucht, damit Sie jetzt dieses starke Heilmittel für zerbrochene Träume genießen können."

Kurz vor seinem Tod erzählte der alte Barkeeper Ray Buhen, einer der Angestellten im Original-Beachcomber im Jahre 1934, die Geschichte noch anders. „Don war ein netter Typ", erinnerte sich Buhen, der 27 Jahre später seine eigene Bar, das Tiki Ti, eröffnete. „Aber er erzählte viel, wenn der Tag lang war. Er hat gesagt, er habe den Zombie erfunden, hat er aber nicht. Und auch kaum einen der anderen Drinks." Buhen war der Meinung, dass die meisten Erfindungen von den „vier Jungs" stammten, einem Filipino-Quartett, die bei Don hinter der Bar arbeiteten. Sicherlich eine ketzerische Behauptung, aber Rays Glaubwürdigkeit ist ziemlich unantastbar: 62 Jahre als Barkeeper in den berühmtesten polynesischen Palästen, von den Seven Seas und dem Luau bis zum China Trader und seiner eigenen Bar, wo er Leute wie Clark Gable, Charlie Chaplin, Buster Keaton, die Marx Brothers und Marlon Brando bediente.

Wie auch immer sie nun entstanden sind, Dons Drinks wurden schnell so populär, dass die „vier Jungs" bald nicht mehr ausreichten. Schließlich hatte er sieben Barmänner, die hauptberuflich bei ihm arbeiteten und alle auf besondere Drinks spezialisiert waren. Hinter ihnen standen noch mehr Filipino-Mitarbeiter, die Ananas mit Stahldraht schälten und zerlegten, riesige Eisblöcke abschabten, bis ihnen die Arme schmerzten, und Limetten auspressten, bis ihnen die Zitronensäure die Fingernägel zerfraß. Und um die Sache auf die Spitze zu treiben, führte er zunächst noch striktere Sicherheitsmaßnahmen ein, um zu verhindern, dass sich diese Assistenten Dons Geheimrezepte merkten. Statt der Etiketten waren die Flaschen nur mit Nummern und Buchstaben gekennzeichnet. Wie einem Artikel in der Saturday Evening Post von 1948 zu entnehmen ist, „sind die Rezepte codiert und die Barkeeper folgen einem vorgegebenen Muster codierter Symbole, mit denen vorgemixte Ingredienzen bezeichnet sind, nicht aber die eigentlichen Namen von Fruchtkonzentraten und Rumsorten. Selbst wenn sich also ein konkurrierender Barbesitzer einen der Beachcomber-Mitarbeiter unter den Nagel reißt ... kann er die Abtrünnige Dons Rezepte nicht mitnehmen." Trotzdem wurde dieses Zombie-Rezept bereits 1941 abgedruckt. Wenn Don der große weiße Vater des tropischen Drinks war, so hatte er viele verlorene Söhne. Kaum hatte Don sein Lokal eröffnet, waren die Nachahmer schon zur Stelle. In Harry Sugerman's Nachtclub *Tropics* in Beverly Hills wurde aus dem *Zombie* der *Zulu*. „One drink, you're impatient! Two drinks, you're impatient! Three drinks, you're impotent!" Während sich einige damit begnügten, Don zu imitieren, hatte sich Trader Vic Größeres vorgenommen. „Ich hatte nicht die geringste Ahnung von diesem ganzen Zeug", schreibt er in seiner Autobiografie, „aber ich dachte, dass ich es gern lernen würde." Er reiste in alle Himmelsrichtungen, um international bekannte Barmänner kennen zu lernen, zum Beispiel Constantine Ribailagua in Havanna (der den Papa Dobles Grapefruit-Daiquiri für Ernest Hemingway kreierte) und Albert Martin in New Orleans (durch Ramos Fizz berühmt). Als er in seine Bar in Oakland zurückkehrte, war Trader Vic längst kein Imitator mehr. Er war ein Erfinder und Erneuerer.

Als Vic den *Scorpion*, den *Samoan Fog Cutter* und den *Mai Tai* erfand, war er plötzlich derjenige, dem man die Ideen klaute. „Davon bekomme ich Magengeschwüre", schnaubte er, wenn er hörte, dass sich Bars von Tahiti bis Tulsa als die Ursprungsorte des *Mai Tai* ausgaben. „Wer behauptet, ich hätte diesen Drink nicht erfunden, ist ein mieses Stinktier." Mit der folgenden für ihn typischen Geschichte rückte er die Legende zurecht: „Eines Tages 1944 stand ich hinter meiner Bar und redete mit meinem Barkeeper, und ich erzählte ihm, dass ich den besten Rumdrink der Welt machen wollte. In dem Augenblick kamen Ham und Carrie Guild, ein paar alte Freunde aus Tahiti, herein. Carrie probierte, hob ihr Glas und sagte, 'Mai Tai – Roa Ae', was auf tahitisch bedeutet, nicht von dieser Welt – einfach der Beste!' Das ist der Name, sagte ich, wir nennen den Drink Mai Tai." Vic's Rezept:

Der Streit darüber, wer den *Mai Tai* erfunden habe, zog sich hin, bis Trader Vic die Angelegenheit vor Gericht brachte und 1970 einen Prozess gegen die Sun-Vac Corporation führte. Zur der Zeit brachte Sun-Vac eine Produktlinie von vorgefertigten Mix-Sirupen heraus, die den Namen „Don the Beachcomber" trug. Ironischerweise behauptete Sun-Vac, dass Don selbst – der Mann, dem Vic, wie er ehrlich zugab, vor dreißig Jahren die Idee geklaut hatte – den Mai Tai erfunden habe. Der Prozess wurde schließlich außergerichtlich zu Vics Gunsten entschieden.

Als die exotischen Rum-Cocktails immer beliebter wurden und die polynesischen Lokale, in denen sie serviert wurden, immer besser liefen, wurde der Wettbewerb natürlich noch erbitterter. Im Gegensatz zu

Don und Vic hatten die neuen Emporkömmlinge noch keine Ruhmestaten vorzuweisen und suchten darum nach irgendeinem Etikett, das ihrem Restaurant das spezielle Markenzeichen verlieh, zum Beispiel indem sie ihre Mitarbeiter zu Cocktail-Wettbewerben schickten, die von Rum-Firmen gesponsert waren. Das Restaurant durfte dann mit seinem eigenen, preisgekrönten Cocktail werben, den sein legendärer Barkeeper kreiert hatte, und die Rum-Firma konnte damit werben, dass das preisgekrönte Rezept mit ihrem Rum gemixt sei.

1953 nahm ein anonymer Kellner aus dem *Luau* beim Pogo Galcini an einem solchen Wettbewerb teil, der von Ron Rico gesponsert war; er gewann und stieg sofort zum Star der Branche auf, obwohl Gerüchte umgingen, dass der Wettbewerb, wie die meisten seiner Art, manipuliert worden sei. Trotzdem wurde Galcini schon bald aus dem *Luau* abgeworben: Im *Kelbo's* in West Los Angeles trat er den ersten einer Reihe lukrativer Auftritte als Barkeeper, bis er schließlich im *Outrigger* in Laguna Beach am Gipfel seiner Karriere angekommen war. Auf der Getränkekarte im *Outrigger* prangte stolz „preisgekrönte Cocktails von POPO".

„Preisgekrönte" Drinks waren aber nicht die einzige Möglichkeit, Tiki-Bars ins Gespräch zu bringen. Wenn man schon nicht die Olivenschaft ins Feld führen konnte, dann zumindest die Kennerschaft.

Nicht länger als minderwertig abgetan, hatte Rum Mitte der 50er Jahre ein völlig neues Image bekommen, was hauptsächlich dem missionarischen Eifer von Vic und Don zu verdanken war, die inzwischen ihre eigenen Marken herstellten und verkauften. Die bessere Gesellschaft sieht in Whiskey und Gin stehen für einen Teufelsrum, der plötzlich zum Drink der „Abenteurer der Meere" und zum „meist diskutierten und sagenumwobenen Getränk aller Zeiten" erklärt und romantisch verbrämt wurde. Wahre Genießer strömten zu den polynesischen Palästen mit ihrer großen Auswahl an seltenen, alten oder sonst wie bemerkenswerten Marken aus allen Teilen der Welt; Restaurantbesitzer rühmten sich ihrer „Rumkeller" oder stellten ihre Riesenauswahl hinter der Bar zur Schau. In seinen Glanzzeiten bot *Don the Beachcomber* 120 verschiedene Rumsorten an. Einige Lokale boten nicht nur eine enorme Auswahl an Rum an, sondern auch ein ebenso gigantisches Angebot an Rum-Cocktails. „Es stehen 36 tropische Drinks zur Auswahl", war in einer Restaurantkritik aus jener über den *China Trader* in Burbank zu lesen, „und ein Professor von der Technischen Universität Kalifornien

stellte einen Rekord auf, indem er sechzehn Drinks schaffte, danach aber vollständig betäubt war." Wir können nur hoffen, dass er das niemals im *Luau* probiert hat, wo nicht weniger als 74 exotische Drinks auf der Karte standen – darunter auch der Martiki, die „polynesische Antwort auf einen trockenen Martini".

In den 60er Jahren strömten selbst die abgehobensten Nachkriegsintellektuellen in Tiki-Bars. Die Regisseure Bob Fosse und Stanley Kubrick waren Stammgäste in New Yorks *Trader Vic's* – wo Kubrick 1964 zum ersten Mal die Idee verlauten ließ, aus der vier Jahre später sein Film „2001: Odyssee im Weltraum" werden sollte. (Wir wissen nicht, was er getrunken hat, aber er muss jenem Professor von der Technischen Universität Konkurrenz gemacht haben.) In seiner Autobiografie erzählt Gore Vidal, dass er den bekannten Historiker Arthur Schlesinger und den Wirtschaftswissenschaftler und Nobelpreisträger John Kenneth Galbraith mit ins *Luau* genommen habe, wo beide, „reichlich mit Rum abgefüllt" mehrere Speichen aus dem riesigen Schiffsrad, das im Eingangsbereich stand, herausbrachen und dabei riefen: „Dies ist das Staatsschiff!" Frank Sinatra war ein großer Fan des *Navy Grog*, den man in *Don the Beachcomber* in Palm Springs servierte. Er war sehr großzügig mit Trinkgeld, erinnert sich Barkeeper Tony Ramos, „aber er kriegte einen Tobsuchtsanfall, wenn er nicht schnell genug bedient wurde".

Als die 70er Jahre zu Ende gingen, änderte sich auch der allgemeine Geschmack. An die Stelle des *Missionary's Downfall* trat jetzt der *Screaming Orgasm* und die besten und erfolgreichsten Barkeeper des goldenen Zeitalters verstreuten sich in alle Winde und nahmen dabei ihr Können, ihre Erfahrung und ihre „geheimen Zutaten" mit. Bittet man heute einen Barkeeper, einen tropischen Drink zu mixen, wird das unangenehm süße Ergebnis leider nur zu oft Tony Ramos' Behauptung bestätigen, dass das Mixen dieser Drinks eine „verlorene Kunst" sei.

Doch auch heute gibt es noch eine Handvoll Lokale, die sich auf gute exotische Drinks verstehen. Das *Mai Kai* in Fort Lauderdale, Florida und das *Kahiki* in Columbus, Ohio, servieren noch immer Mystery Drinks in verzierten Schalen, die von spärlich bekleideten Eingeborenenmädchen zum Klang von zeremoniellen Gongs serviert werden. Und das *Tiki Ti* des verstorbenen Ray Buhen, das unter seinem Sohn Mike geführt wird, bietet den Einwohnern von Los Angeles immer noch 72 einwandfrei gemixte exotische Drinks. Wie könnte man dieses Kapitel über die

Geschichte amerikanischer Drinks besser schließen als mit Rays Worten: „Es ist Eskapismus. Es ist nicht real. Es ist ein Riesen-Tam-Tam", sagte er über die so genannten polynesischen Cocktails. Und dann: „Oh ja, das waren noch Zeiten".

... UND DIE GÖTTER WAREN GUTER DINGE

Hawaii, 1820, ein Tanzfest. Der Missionar Hiram Bingham beobachtet die Eingeborenen bei einem Hula-Marathon, wie sie einem Götterkopf Leis (Blumengirlanden) zum Geschenk machen, und er versucht, sie zu verstehen. „Wozu dient euch ein er Gott, wofür ist er gut?" Ihre einfache Antwort verwirrt ihn: „Zum Spielen." Ein Konzept, das damals für den Puritaner noch völlig unzugänglich war, sollte ein Jahrhundert später den den Amerikanern auf fruchtbaren Boden fallen sollte. Ihre Rechtschaffenheit und Bescheidenheit hatte ihnen geholfen, die Depression durchzustehen und den Zweiten Weltkrieg zu gewinnen. Ein gesicherter Lebensstandard schien für jeden erreichbar zu sein, und nun war die Zeit gekommen, zu spielen. Doch die unerschütterlichen Moralvorstellungen der Väter, die diesem Bedürfnis im Wege standen, waren schwer abzuschütteln. Es musste eine alternative Welt geschaffen werden, in der man in eine freizügigere Rolle schlüpfen konnte. Die polynesische sorglose Kultur Polynesiens wurde zum Vorbild einer eskapistischen Gegenwelt. Wo immer man Spaß haben konnte, da herrschte Tiki.

Durch die vielfältigen Konzepte, die zur Unterhaltung der Gäste verwirklicht wurden, waren Tiki-Bars richtige kleine Vergnügungszentren geworden. Daher war es eine natürliche Entwicklung, Tiki-Tempel in Spielparks zu integrieren oder eigene Tiki-Parks zu bauen. Die Ferienparadiese Kaliforniens und Florida boten den richtige Kombination aus Erholungswert und Klima, und so entstanden solche Tiki-Welten wie Tiki Gardens und The Tikis. Der Big Kahuna der Vergnügungsparks, Walt Disney, wollte dem natürlich in nichts nachstehen. Als häufiger Gast in polynesischen Nachtclubs hatte er beschlossen, ein Tiki-Restaurant zu eröffnen, das alle bisher existierenden in den Schatten stellen sollte. Walt war ein Animationskünstler und daher war für ihn der nächste logische Schritt, den ganzen üblichen Schmuck als Blumen, Vögeln und Tikis lebendig werden zu lassen. Der Geist Tikis inspirierte Disney, das Konzept der „Audio-Animatronics" zu entwickeln, das später zum Herzstück vieler Disneyland-Attraktionen wurde. Doch als das Projekt sich seiner Vollendung näherte, war die Raumzeitaltertechnologie von

225 Roboterdarstellern, die von einem Vierzehnkanal-Magnetband gesteuert wurden, das an hundert separate Lautsprecher angeschlossen war und 438 Handlungen kontrollierte, über den zur Verfügung stehenden Raum des Restaurants hinausgewachsen, und anstatt einen Kompromiss einzugehen und die ganze Show etwas zu reduzieren, beschloss Walt, den Gastronomiebereich zu streichen und aus der Show eine eigenständige Attraktion zu machen. Als The Enchanted Tiki Room 1963 eröffnet wurde, schrieb die New York Times: „POLARIS-TONBAND HILFT DISNEY-ANIMATION – Neues Synchronisiergerät lässt Totempfähle sprechen ... Im Enchanted Tiki Room reden, singen und pfeifen Dutzende von leuchtenden bunten synthetischen Vögeln. Geschnitzte heidnische Götter schlagen Trommeln und singen in fremdartigen Lauten. Stürme brausen und Quellen plätschern. Künstliche Papageien führen in verschiedenen Dialekten Gespräche."

In seiner begeisterten, wenn auch recht intellektuellen Besprechung „SPIEL, PARADOX UND MENSCHENMENGEN: EHRFURCHT IN DISNEYLAND", in der er den Enchanted Tiki Room mit anderen von Menschen gebauten „Kraft-Zentren" verglich, schrieb Stanford-Professor Don D. Jackson, Direktor des Palo Alto Mental Research Institute: „... und zwar weil ich behaupte, ebenso viel Ehrfurcht, Verwunderung und Verehrung empfunden zu haben, als ich in dem synthetischen, technisch konstruierten, instant-polynesischen Tiki-Room in Disneyland saß, wie ich es in einigen der großen Kathedralen – Chartres, Rheims und Notre Dame – erlebt habe ..."

Eine andere Form des Familienvergnügungscenters, die mit dem Tiki-Thema zu tun hatte, war die Bowlingbahn. Meistens war es die angrenzende Cocktailbar, manchmal aber auch das gesamte Establissement, das dem Gott der Erholung gewidmet war. Bowling hatte seinen Ursprung in deutschen Klöstern, wo Mönche die Kirchgänger einen flaschenförmigen Gegenstand umhauen ließen, um dadurch ihre fromme Ergebenheit zu Gott zu bekunden. Der hölzerne Kegel stellte den Teufel dar, und ihn umzustürzen bedeutete völlige Erlösung von den Sünden. Es ist nicht bekannt, ob je tikiförmige Bowlingkegel existiert haben, doch in vielen Lokalen wurden Aloha-Hemden und Bowling-Hemden beliebig gemischt und tropische Getränke sorgten dafür, den Tiki-Nachtschwärmern ihr Ziel klarer vor Augen zu führen. Einer dieser Orte war das extravagante Kapu Kai (Verbotenes Meer) in Rancho Cucamonga, einem Vorort von Los Angeles. Vier Eingänge in dynamisch aufragender A-Form

lockten die Gläubigen an. Die Tikis zwischen den Kegelbahnen und um das Gebäude herum wären von Milan Guanko geschnitzt. Die Relief-Tikis auf der Eingangstür begrüßten die ankommenden Gäste mit einem Lächeln, innen aber zeigen sie den Hinausgehenden einen Schmollmund. Die Böden waren mit Tiki-Teppichen ausgelegt und der „tahitische Feuerraum" stellte beeindruckende Tapa-Wandbehänge zur Schau. Und doch war alles schnell vorbei – trotz seines bemerkenswerten Designs überlebte das Kapu Kai nicht das Ende des 20. Jahrhunderts.

HOTEL, MOTEL

Im Amerika der 60er Jahren gingen Tourismus und Tikis Hand in Hand, und da die Motel-Leuchtreklamen die Totempfähle der amerikanischen Straßenrandkultur waren, wurden Tikis oft als Blickfang eingesetzt. Sie waren Leuchttürme im Stadtozean und ihre Tiki-Fackeln, mit Neon oder Gas betrieben, dienten als Leuchtfeuer für müde Reisende und moderne Kaufleute – Polynesien war nun mit dem Auto erreichbar. Das Motel war eine amerikanische Variante des Hotels, das eigens für die vierrädrige hatte Kult geschaffen werden war. Der Himmel war die Grenze für amerikanische Autobauer jener Zeit, Größe und Aussehen Ihrer Produkte erreichten die Dimensionen von Raumschiffen. Für diese mussten leicht zugängliche Anlegeplätze geschaffen werden, mit einem dazu passenden Ort, an dem sich ihre Kapitäne bis zum nächsten Auslaufen ausruhen konnten. Um diese Raumschiffhäfen in unübersichtlichen Stadtuniversum kenntlich zu machen, wurden riesige Leuchtreklamen am Rande der Hauptverkehrsadern errichtet.

Seither ist die Motel-Leuchtreklame ein klassisches Symbol amerikanischer Kultur. Es ist daher ein wirkliches Zeichen von Ignoranz, dass Anaheim, Heimatstadt Disneylands, Anziehungspunkt für Touristen aus aller Welt auf der Suche nach amerikanischer Popkultur, noch 1998 die Motel-Leuchtreklame des Pitcairn im Rahmen ihrer „Verschönerungskampagne" abreißen ließ. Es scheint, dass Kulturikonen am ehesten dann Gefahr laufen, abgerissen oder zerstört zu werden, wenn ihr Wert gerade kurz vor der Wiederentdeckung steht. Folglich ist absehbar, dass es bald schlechte Imitationen solcher Leuchtreklamen geben wird, die dann in einigen Jahren in Disneyland aufgestellt werden, direkt neben den nachgebauten Diners, ausgestattet mit Autoteilen aus den 50er Jahren. So ist das Hanalei-Zeichen in San Diego ein perfektes Beispiel für „vorher" und „nachher" und die Ignoranz einer Firma, die der Modernität zuliebe den individuellen Ausdruck durch eine alles beherrschende Unverbindlichkeit ersetzen lässt. Genau wie bei dem ikonenhaften *Stardust*-Zeichen in Las Vegas, das auch durch eine fade Standard-Schrifttype ersetzt wurde, die nichts mehr mit dem Weltraumthema zu tun hat.

Tiki-Motels waren in ganz Amerika, nicht nur in klimatisch milderen Zonen, beliebt. Um das Hauptgebäude des *Tiki Motor Inn* in Lake George im Staat New York standen künstliche Palmen, die selbst im Schnee noch grün waren. Die einzig wahre Tiki-Motelkette jedoch entstand in den kalifornischen Wüstenstädten: Ken Kimes betrieb einst vierzig Motels, von denen fünf mit Tikis aus der Werkstatt von Oceanic Arts ausgestattet waren: Die *Tropics* in Indio, Blythe, Rosemead, Modesto und Palm Springs. Vier davon beherbergen noch immer Tikis, die durch das trockene Klima gut erhalten sind. Das *Tropics* in Palm Springs ist Tiki-Stil in Vollendung, wenngleich seine „Reef"-Bar erst kürzlich im mexikanischen Stil umgestaltet worden ist. Die Wiederentdeckung von Palm Springs als Zentrum der Moderne in der Mitte des 20. Jahrhunderts wird hoffentlich dazu beitragen, dass dieser außerordentliche Tiki-Tempel erhalten bleibt.

FÜR DEN JUNGGESELLEN EINE BEISPIELLOSE UMGEBUNG

„Überquere die handgeschnitzte Fußgängerbrücke, die über den Abgrund der Göttin Pele führt, wo die Lava kurz vor dem Ausbruch steht und die Erde gleich zu beben beginnen wird, dann befindest du dich in der besten Gegend aller Welten, fern von Stress, Sorgen und Nöten; und doch nur Minuten entfernt von öffentlichen Verkehrsmitteln, Kirchen, und nur Sekunden entfernt vom Festland ... In dieser fantastischen Umgebung weiß Pele alles. Sie gehörte und wird immer in den Pantheon der hawaiischen Götter gehören. Du kannst dich entspannen und in der Sonne liegen, es gibt dafür einen palmenbestandenen Schwimmbereich mit Wasser, das aus der Korallenquelle in die schön geformte Lagune sprudelt. Auf der Fußgängerbrücke im Inneren stehst du dann inmitten der Ruinen ihres Reiches, wo die Überreste von Hopoe und Lohiau, in zwei riesige Felsen verwandelt, im wilden Wasser stehen, das in Kaskaden von den lavabedeckten Hang eines brodelnden Vulkans herabstürzt. Von den Göttern getröstet kannst du hier dein Heim aufschlagen, in der herrlichen, palmenbestandenen und für den Junggesellen beispiellosen Umgebung leben ..."

Dieses eindrückliche Beispiel für polynesische Pop-Poesie aus der Werbebroschüre der *Pele*-Apartments gibt eine gute Vorstellung davon, wie viel Mühe sich die Erbauer gegeben haben, diese „polynesischen" Wohnblöcke zu gestalten. Die architektonischen Entwürfe griffen auf alles zurück, was Tiki-Restaurants und Freizeitlokale bisher geboten hatten. Im speziellen Fall der *Pele*-Apartments wurde der Broschürentext vom Cover einer beliebten Exotica-Platte kopiert.

Der Erbauer des *Pele*-Apartments entwickelte ein ansprechendes Design-Konzept für Apartmentwohnungen in seinem *Shelter Isle*-Wohnkomplex, das in seinen Werbebroschüren den bevorstehenden Niedergang der Tiki-Kultur zu erahnen schien: „Wenn man den Erholungsbereich verlässt und gemächlich die gewundenen Pfade entlang schlendert, findet man sich plötzlich in den Ruinen eines verlassenen Dorfes wieder. Hier stehen die Überreste einer Eingeborenensiedlung einsam an einem kleinen See, der von wilden Wassern gespeist wird, die von den lavabedeckten Hängen eines brodelnden Vulkans herabstürzen."

Als Stadtarchäologen Mitte der 90er Jahre diese Einrichtung entdeckten, waren von diesen „Überresten" nur einige überwachsene Lava-Felsen neben einem Teich übrig geblieben. Zumeist bieten Tiki-Dörfer dem Archäologen der Tiki-Kultur allerdings ergiebigere Einsichten, denn im allgemeinen haben sie die Abschaffung der Götzenverehrung besser überlebt als ihre Vorfahren, die Restaurants und Lounges. Da sie nicht so abhängig von Veränderungen des Geschmacks sind wie die Restaurantkultur, stellen sie manchmal regelrechte Refugien jener bedrohten Spezies der Tikis dar.

Auch wenn manche Besitzer und Pächter versucht haben, sie mit missionarischem Eifer in einen zeitgemäßen Zustand zu versetzen, und viele Tikis verrottet oder von Grabräubern gestohlen worden sind, kann man beim Durchforsten des Stadtgebiets von Los Angeles nach hohen Palmen und A-Form-Bauten noch immer spektakuläre Entdeckungen zutage fördern. Im *Tahitian Village* im San Fernando Valley sind die Archetypen für Feuer und Wasser durch zwei Eingeborenenskulpturen im Stile Gauguins dargestellt, die die Eingangsbrücke flankieren. Die männliche Figur spie einst Wasser aus dem Mund in ihre Hände und lies es von dort in den Graben unter der Brücke fließen; die weibliche Figur hielt eine offene Gasflamme in der Hand. Eine über zwei Meter hohe Betonmaske, Tiki-Stützpfosten und überall Eisengeländer mit einem Dekor aus gekreuzten Speeren mit Schild sind weitere Besonderheiten dieser Wohnanlage.

Die Tiki-Fackeln im *Polynesian Village* in Playa del Rey brennen nicht mehr und ebenso wenig die Vulkanfeuer, die aus dem großen Wasserfall hervorbrachen. Aber die eigenwillig geschnitzten Einbaumbalken, die tropische Landschaftsgestaltung und die heterogene Lavafelsen- und Betonarchitektur von Armet & Davis geben immer noch ein hervorragendes Beispiel für einen Stil ab, der sich entwickelte, als es erstrebenswert erschien, wie ein Primitiver, aber in der Nähe eines modernen Flughafen zu wohnen, als Flugreisen noch bezauberend waren und mit dem Jetset gleichgesetzt wurden, anstatt mit Lärm, Luftverpestung und Reisestress: „Stromlinienförmige beschwingt, luxuriös und elegant, ein Spiegel des Düsenzeitalters, sind kunstvoll mit dem Kolorit, der Romantik und dem Zauber der Südseeinseln angereichert, um eine verführerische Umgebung nach neuestem Design in den *Playa del Ray Polynesian*-Apartments zu schaffen ... Geschnitzte Tiki-Götter wachen über die üppigen, herrlich gestalteten Gartenlandschaft und lassen ihren Zauber wirken, um Gesundheit, Glück und Zufriedenheit zu bringen."

Wie die Tempel waren auch die Dörfer am weitesten in Kalifornien verbreitet, blieben jedoch nicht auf wärmere Gegenden beschränkt. Entlang der ganzen Westküste, rund um Seattle in Tacoma und Bremerton, einer Navy-Werftstadt, wurden viele Tiki-Wohnanlagen gebaut. Über ganz Amerika verstreut bildeten sich mehr oder weniger exquisite Gemeinschaften, die dem Gott der Erholung huldigten. Die Namen dieser Vorstadtinseln waren genauso vielsagend wie der Schriftstil ihrer Schilder. Ob sie *Beachcomber*, *Asian*, *Primitive*, *Bamboo* oder *Fat Samoan* hießen – all diese Schriften waren Teil der Tiki-Ästhetik. Bestimmte Flügel oder Bereiche der Wohnanlagen hatten spezielle Bezeichnungen wie „Snug Harbour" oder „Mauna Loa", benannt nach Orten oder Hotels auf Hawaii.

Die *Exotic Isle*-Appartements in Alhambra, einem Vorort von Los Angeles, die heute überwiegend von asiatischen Emigranten bewohnt werden, waren bis vor kurzem noch sehr eindrucksvolle Dokumente des Tiki-Kultes. Ein Entspannungsraum, der sich über den Hauptwasserfall erstreckt, bildet das Zentrum und könnte als Tiki-Entsprechung für Frank Lloyd Wrights *Falling Water* angesehen werden.

POLYNESIEN VOR DER EIGENEN HAUSTÜR

In mehr als einer Hinsicht war das Bedürfnis des Durchschnittsamerikaners, „den Wilden zu spielen", eine Regression in die Kindheit. Die Verantwortung bei der Arbeit und in der Familie ließ sich am besten bei „Luau"-Gartenpartys vergessen; einer Art Geburtstagsparty für „große Jungs", wo Spaß und Spiele wieder erlaubt waren. Erwachsene Weiße in blumigen Hawaiihemden oder „MUU MUU"-Kleidern konsumierten süßes Essen und noch süßere Drinks, die weiter dazu beitragen, den Intellekt auf Kinderniveau herabzuschrauben, übten sich im Hula-Tanz und im melodiösen, konsonantenlosen Singsang der hawaiischen Sprache: „Alle KANES, WAHINES und KEIKIS (Männer, Frauen und Kinder) wollen WIKI WIKI (eilen) zu einem hawaiischen LUAU (Fest). MALIHINIS (Neuankömmlinge) wollen die Bedeutung der seltsamen Wörter kennen lernen, die sie erst zum Luau hören. Wahines tragen HOLOKUS (hawaiisches Prinzessinnengewand mit Schleppe) oder MUU MUUS (flatternde Gewänder mit Blumenmuster). Kanes tragen ALOHA-Hemden (fröhliche Sporthemden). Ein PAPALE (Hut) ist nicht nötig. ALOHA (Begrüßung) bringt man dadurch zum Ausdruck, dass man eine LEI (Blumengirlande) um den Hals der Malihini legt. Das Luau wird an langen Tischen serviert, die auf einer LANAI (offener Veranda) oder unter dem Palmenbaldachin im Hof stehen. Das Essen wird in einem IMU (unterirdischer Ofen) gekocht, für den man ein LUA (Loch) in die Erde gräbt und es mit POHAKU (Steinen) und KUNI (Zündmaterial) füllt. Man macht ein AHI (Feuer), um die Pohaku zu erhitzen. Das PUA (Schwein), das im Imu gegart wird, heißt PUA KALUA. Wenn das Luau ein AHAAINA (großes Fest) ist, dauert es Stunden, bis es PAU (beendet) ist und alle HIAMOE (schlafen) gehen. Der Schlaf kommt schnell, denn der OPU (Bauch) fühlt sich angenehm an von so viel KAU KAU (Essen)."

Imu-Löcher wurden in den Gärten ausgehoben, als sei der Goldrausch zurückgekehrt, doch allein der Wunsch, zum Wilden zu werden, war nicht genug. Die entsprechende Dekoration musste her. Die notwendigen Utensilien, um diese Happenings auszustatten, konnte man in Baumschulen und Spezialgeschäften wie „Sea and Jungle" im Valley, bei „Oceanic Arts" in Whittier oder bei „Johnson Products" in Chicago finden. Tiki-Fackeln, Grasmatten, Palmwedel, Bambusstöcke, Fischernetze, Speere und Trommeln und alles, was es in Tiki-Form gab, war hier zu bekommen. So baute man Tiki-Hütten in Hinterhöfen und Gärten und stellte Götzenbilder an Swimmingpools und auf Veranden auf, und die Tikis wurden zu den neuen Gartenzwergen der Vereinigten Staaten.

Für den Hobbybastler gab es komplette Bausätze mit Anleitung, wie man sich seine eigene Tiki-Bar bauen konnte. In vielen Vorstadthäusern wurden die Kellerräume in Partykeller umgewandelt, in denen sich Erwachsene zu Cocktailpartys und „Erwachsenengesprächen" trafen. Wenn Hattan- und Bambusmöbel nicht genug Eindruck machten, dann schafften es sicherlich die mit geschnitzten Tikis verzierten Bars und Stühle aus dem Haus Witco. Elvis Presley, immer ein sicherer Maßstab in Sachen Volksgeschmack, stattete seinen „Jungle Room" in Graceland mit Witco-Möbeln aus. Elvis schwamm mit auf dem Höhepunkt der polynesischen Welle mit seinen Filmen „Blaues Hawaii", „Südseeparadies" und „Clambake", in dem die großartigste Luau-Szene am Strand von Florida zu sehen ist, die es je in einem Film gab.

DIE KÜNSTLER

Die Schöpfer der bisher nicht anerkannten Kunstform des modernen Tiki-Stils, amerikanische Tiki-Bildhauer, sind niemals als Künstler akzeptiert worden. Ihre Produkte wurden als „authentisch" bezeichnet, ein verschwommener Begriff, der Echtheit bedeuten kann, aber nicht zwingend beschreibt, dass es sich um Originale handelt. Keiner wollte die Aufmerksamkeit darauf lenken, dass etwa die dunkle Haut des Holzschnitzers Vince Buono daher rührte, dass er einer New Yorker Immigrantenfamilie italienischen Ursprungs entstammte und nicht von einer Südseeinsel. Tiki-Stil hatte nichts mit mutwilligem Betrug zu tun, er bediente nur das Bedürfnis des Publikums nach Selbstbetrug, und daher hüllte er sich und seine Schöpfer in Geheimnisse. Die Motorsäge, die Leroy Schmaltz schwingt, war tabu bei öffentlichen Auftritten, wo die Schnitzarbeit mit Hammer und Meisel vorgeführt wurde. In diesem Kapitel soll einigen Künstlern, stellvertretend für alle, die unbekannt bleiben, die gebührende Anerkennung zuteil werden.

Leroy Schmaltz und Bob van Oosting gründeten ihre Dekorationsfirma „Oceanic Arts" in Whittier, einem Vorort von Los Angeles, in den späten 50er Jahren, auf dem Höhepunkt der Tiki-Begeisterung. Sie hatten ganz klein mit Tiki-Amuletten und Palmwedelmasken begonnen. Doch schnell entwickelte sich „Oceanic Arts" zum größten landesweiten Hersteller und Vertreiber von Tiki-Kunst und Einrichtungsmaterial. Alle großen Restaurantketten von Don the Beachcomber bis Kon-Tiki arbeiteten mit ihnen zusammen, und bei der Masse an Aufträgen war praktisch jeder Holzschnitzer der Branche irgendwann einmal bei ihnen beschäftigt. Manchmal wurden die Tikis von den Architekten oder Innenaus-

stattern entworfen, meistens aber folgten die Holzschnitzer ihren eigenen Ideen und biswellen übernahmen sie sogar die komplette Innenausstattung der Lokale.

Die Liste der Auftragsarbeiten im „Oceanic Arts" ist lang, denn sie hatten mit den meisten Tiki-Tempeln zu tun, die in diesem Buch dargestellt sind. Vom Kahiki in Ohio über das Mai Kai in Florida bis zum The Tikis in Monterey Park (Kapitel 10) kann man „Oceanic Arts"-Produkte in ganz Amerika entdecken. Selbst das amerikante Bishop Museum in Honolulu beherbergt einige ihrer Schnitzwerke, wenn auch nicht in den Ausstellungsvitrinen, so doch an den Wänden der Cafeteria. Für das kulturübergreifende Phänomen des Tiki-Stils schloss sich der Kreis, als Götzenbilder aus der Werkstatt von „Oceanic Arts" für Hotels und Restaurants auf Hawaii, Samoa und Tahiti exportiert wurden. Heute ist „Oceanic Arts" der größte Hersteller von polynesischen Schmuckartikeln, der den Niedergang der Tiki-Kultur erfolgreich überlebt hat und eine neue Forschergeneration aus aller Welt an die Gestade von Whittier, Kalifornien, lockt.

Nördlich von San Francisco, im malerischen Jachthafen von Sausalito, hat der Ex-Offizier der Handelsmarine, Barney West, sein Lager mit seinem „Tiki Junction" aufgeschlagen. Er fand zu seiner Berufung als er im Zweiten Weltkrieg auf den Marianen strandete. Zu seinem „Tiki Junction"-Logo inspirierte ihn ein Buch, das aus lässlich der ersten Ausstellung von Südseekunst in Amerika im Jahre 1946 veröffentlicht wurde; das Trader Vic-Logo soll auch hierauf zurückzuführen sein. Trader Vic, der sein Geschäft auf der anderen Seite der Bucht in Emeryville nahe Oakland hatte, wurde der Hauptkunde für Barneys Tikis. Noch heute finden sich einige dieser Götzenbilder, die seinen unverwechselbaren Stil aufweisen, in vielen Trader Vic's-Filialen rund um die Welt. Barney entspricht ganz der Rolle des trinkfesten, frauenverschleißenden Bohemien, und er ist schon lange in den Tiki-Himmel eingegangen.

Milan Guanko lernte das Schnitzen schon als Kind von seinem Vater auf den Philippinen. Nachdem er 1928 in die Vereinigten Staaten ausgewandert war und im Lebensmittelhandel gearbeitet hatte, fand er seine Nische in der aufkeimenden Polynesienbegeisterung. Schließlich wurde er einer der produktivsten und einflussreichsten Tiki-Schnitzer in Amerika, sein Stil wurde kopiert und für den wachsenden Bedarf der Tiki-Anhänger vermarktet. Zu seinen Kunden gehören The Islands in Phoenix, Arizona, das Kapu Kai in Rancho Cucamonga und Ren Clarks Polynesian Village in Fort Worth, Texas, für das Guanko und zwei mexikanische Schnitzer, Juan Razo und Fidel Rodriguez (die das *Mauna Loa* in Mexico City ausgestattet hatten), mehr als zweihundert Tikis geschnitzt haben, manche in Form von Barhockern, andere als dreieinhalb Meter hohe Riesen. 1960 war es ein polynesisches Vorzeigeparadies, heute ist von diesem künstlichen Tiki-Wald nichts übrig geblieben und der Verbleib seiner vielen Bewohner ist unbekannt.

In William Westenhavers Witco-Welt war nur ein geschnitztes Stück Holz ein gutes Stück Holz. Ob er seine „Plüschteppich-Brenn-Reliefs" oder komplette Schlafzimmereinrichtungen im primitiven Stil kreierte – keine glatte Fläche entging der Kettensäge dieses Verrückten. Wo immer er ein Tiki-Gesicht anbringen konnte, flogen die Holzspäne. Dann wurde das Holz mit einem Schweißbrenner angeflammt, um die Maserung in dicken schwarzen Adern sichtbar zu machen. Aber es war nicht nur polynesische Pop-Kunst, auch moderner und Konquistadoren-Raumdekor wurde in der Witco-Fabrik in Seattle am Fließband produziert. Eine Zeit lang hatte Witco Ausstellungsräume in Chicago, Dallas, Denver und Seattle und Westenhavers Kunst findet sich noch immer in Motels in Florida und in Trödelläden überall in den Vereinigten Staaten. Zu seinen Kunden gehörten Elvis Presley und Hugh Hefner. Sogar einige „Häuser von schlechtem Ruf" sollen bei ihm Kunden gewesen sein. Zu seinen gelungensten Arbeiten gehören etliche Tiki-Bars und Tiki-Springbrunnen.

Der Autor dieses Buches arbeitet derzeit an einer Monografie über das umfangreiche Schaffen dieses originellen Kunsthandwerkers. Zu guter Letzt möchte er seine Hoffnung zum Ausdruck bringen, dass das vorliegende Buch dazu beitragen mag, der Tiki-Kultur die ihr gebührende Anerkennung zu verschaffen.

FRANÇAIS

TIKI STYLE. LE CULTE DU POP POLYNÉSIEN DANS L'AMERIQUE DES ANNÉES 50

LE GUIDE DE L'ARCHEOLOGUE URBAIN. DÉCOUVRIR UNE CIVILISATION PERDUE DEVANT SA PORTE

« La putréfaction se répand parmi les idoles – le fruit sur leurs autels devient insultant – les temples ont besoin d'une renaissance... » (Herman Melville : *Taïpi*, 1846)

Ces remarques sur le destin de l'ancienne civilisation polynésienne, tirées de l'un des classiques de la littérature inspirée par les mers du Sud, semblent étonnamment appropriées pour accorder compte du sort qui a frappé le style tiki américain des années 1950 et 1960. Ses symboles, les tiki, sont en décrépitude, la cuisine polynésienne de cette époque est devenue l'antithèse de l'alimentation saine, et la plupart des exemples de l'architecture tiki qui ont survécu semblent délabrés. Mais, de même que Paul Gauguin était fasciné par l'atmosphère mélancolique du déclin de Papeete, la capitale de Tahiti, repérant « la surface trouble d'une énigme insondable » dans ce paradis déjà corrompu, l'archéologue urbain d'aujourd'hui reconnaît les vestiges de ce « Paradis perdu » de la dolce vita américaine que nous appelons le style tiki.

Les temples tiki, que l'on rencontrait jadis dans toute ville américaine d'importance, ont disparu, ou bien ont été rénovés, les « grossières images à l'aspect jovial » chassées avec un zèle missionnaire pour faire place aux nouveaux dieux (ou styles). Les cascades ont cessé de couler comme le mana qui avait permis leur installation, les torches tiki ont disparu et les poutres saillantes ont été sectionnées. Mais l'archéologue des villes a développé une sensibilité exacerbée pour les cultures disparues et leurs formes oubliées. Ignorant la peur, il explore leurs sites dans des lieux aussi exotiques que Colombus, l'Ohio ou Pomona, dans la mer urbaine de Los Angeles. Pour lui, s'immerger dans quelque secrète voie express jusqu'à une super périphérie non répertoriée, un jour de pollution, est aussi excitant que de naviguer à bord du Kon-Tiki au sein du Pacifique déchaîné. Tel un batteur de grève intégral, il passe au crible des débris de la culture de consommation dans des dépôts-vente, les débarras d'arrière-cours et les bouquinistes. Tout cela pour compléter le puzzle de modes de vie disparus qui ont engendré des concepts tels que celui du Paradis Polynésien Urbain. Avec un émerveillement intact, l'archéologue urbain découvre qu'il ne faut pas chercher bien loin pour explorer les mystères de traditions disparues, et que d'étranges trésors peuvent se trouver à notre porte, enfouis sous les couches du progrès et du développement. Nous voulons, à travers ce livre, entretenir chez vous cette faculté à reconnaître le merveilleux dans l'apparente banalité, offrir un guide de la culture tiki en Amérique.

AU COMMENCEMENT ...

Depuis qu'il an a été chassé, l'homme a toujours aspiré à retrouver le chemin du paradis. Les premiers récits sur les îles des mers du Sud apparus dans l'Ancien Monde semblaient décrire ce havre perdu. La Polynésie devint la métaphore de l'Eden sur terre. Mais comme ses rivages lointains étaient inaccessibles au commun des mortels, les explorateurs se mirent en quête d'autres terres mythiques.

L'une d'elle était la Californie, une île mystérieuse (on croyait alors qu'il s'agissait d'un continent) que l'on croyait peuplée d'amazones. Même lorsque cette terra incognita fut colonisée et que ces débordements d'imagination se révélèrent terriblement excessif, la Californie conserva son statut de pays de rêve. Des générations et des générations s'établirent, cherchant à réaliser leur propre version du paradis. L'une de ces interprétations édéniques était le jardin tropical des îles des mers du Sud.

Le premier palmier fut planté et la flore tropicale se propagea. Et comme la biosphère tout autant que la psychosphère étaient parfaitement adaptées, une Polynésie américaine vit très vite le jour. On érigea des temples tiki et les gens crurent un temps à ces idoles. Ils célébraient le culte du primitivisme moderne, pratiquant avec ferveur des rites aujourd'hui tabous tels que l'alcoolisme, le racisme, la phallocratie et la consommation de viande de porc. Et de même que les Californiens imitaient la Polynésie, le reste de la nation trouvait en Californie le modèle d'un style de vie. Bientôt, chaque ville importante des Etats-Unis abrita au moins un palais polynésien.

TIKI – QUI ETAIT-IL ?

Au commencement était le Verbe, et le Verbe était : « tik » ! C'est du moins ce que prétendait l'expert en ethnolinguistique, Merrit Ruhlen de Palo Alto, Californie. Il faisait remonter l'origine de tout langage humain à ce mot magique de trois lettres, qui survit aujourd'hui dans l'américain

« digit » (et bien entendu dans l'argot français « trique »). Doté d'un tel pouvoir archaïque, il n'est guère surprenant que « tiki » soit devenu le cri de ralliement de toute une génération.

Mais « tiki » n'était pas seulement proche du premier mot proféré par l'humanité, il est également synonyme du premier homme dans la mythologie polynésienne. D'après le « Concise Maori Dictionary » d'A. W. Reed, cela s'explique ainsi :

1. TIKI : Le premier homme, ou la personnification de l'homme. A travers le culte ancestral, cet Adam maori devint un demi-dieu, et finalement le terme « tiki » fut utilisé dans toutes les descriptions de l'homme, comme nous le voyons dans sa signification suivante :

2. TIKI : La sculpture grotesque de l'homme dans une maison. Une description concise du type de tiki que nous trouvons dans ce livre. Mais, poursuivant la lecture, le mot révèle une signification encore plus profonde.

3. TIKI : Un symbole phallique. En effet, dans la culture maori, tiki désigne la puissance procréatrice et l'organe sexuel du dieu Tane, créateur de la première femme. Dans les îles Australes, au sud de Tahiti, « tiki-roa » (la longue figure ancestrale) était le surnom du pénis, et « tiki-poto » (la courte figure ancestrale) désignait affectueusement le clitoris.

Ce mot ayant de tels pouvoirs créatifs, nous ne sommes pas surpris de lui trouver déjà une autre signification dans les îles Marquises :

4. TIKI : Le dieu des artistes. Montrer que Tiki inspira en effet de nombreux artistes, connus et inconnus, est l'une des ambitions de ce livre, qu'il puisse aussi s'établir comme le protecteur très attendu des artistes.

L'ART PRIMITIF DANS LES LIEUX CIVILISES

« Quiconque les a vus, se trouve ensuite hanté comme par un rêve fiévreux. » (Karl Woermann, à propos des tiki, dans son « Geschichte der Kunst aller Zeiten und Völker, 1900–1911).

L'esthétique apparemment naïve et sauvage de l'art dit « primitif » pour adoucir les lignes du design moderne a été une source d'inspiration pour les fondateurs de l'art moderne. Lorsque, au début du XXe siècle, de plus en plus de « curiosités artificielles » (objets d'art d'Afrique et d'Océanie) arrivèrent des colonies dans les villes de l'Europe occidentale, une nouvelle génération d'artistes tels que Picasso, Miro, Klee et Ernst, s'en inspirèrent pour défier les canons artistiques en vigueur à l'époque. Comme le note Gauguin, l'étude des

arts classiques établis « me dégoûtait et me décourageait, me donnant un vague sentiment de mort sans renaissance ». Pablo Picasso eut une révélation (« … soudain, j'ai compris pourquoi j'étais un peintre ! ») en découvrant la collection d'art primitif du Musée d'Ethnographie du Trocadéro. En fait, dès 1919, il était célébré comme un « vieil adepte du tiki », et ce probablement parce qu'il était depuis 1910 le fier propriétaire d'un tiki des Marquises qui l'accompagna tout au long de son inégalable carrière.

Alors que l'art primitif fut essentiellement apprécié par l'avant-garde durant les années 1920 et 1930, il séduisit la classe moyenne après la Seconde Guerre mondiale. On l'associait désormais à un style de vie artistique, bohème et à une conception de l'existence originale et ludique. A la fin des années 1950, on se devait de posséder une œuvre d'art tribale surprenante pour rompre un tant soit peu la monotonie du décor de son salon contemporain. L'heure du tiki avait sonné.

LE PRE-TIKI ET LA NAISSANCE DU POP POLYNESIEN

« Oh, être né sur l'une des îles des mers du Sud tel un soi-disant sauvage, pour, une fois seulement, jouir de l'existence humaine dans toute sa pureté et sans arrière-pensée. » (Conversations de Goethe avec Eckermann, 12.3.1828)

Le désir d'échanger les bienfaits de la civilisation contre un mode de vie plus simple et plus naturel est aussi ancien que la « civilisation » elle-même. Les rêveurs comme les philosophes sérieux considéraient que les premiers récits de voyages de Cook et Bougainville racontant leurs expéditions dans les mers du Sud, décrivaient l'alternative parfaite aux conditions de vie prévalant dans la société artificielle de la vieille Europe. Melville a célébré dans « Taïpi » le naturel des femmes indigènes : « J'aurais aimé voir, à l'Abbaye de Westminster, nos beautés de la cour face à ces filles des îles. Leur raideur, leur air formel et affecté, auraient produit un saisissant contraste avec la vivacité et la grâce naturelle de ces femmes sauvages. »

Le doux climat, la beauté sans artifices, des indigènes ardents, et les nourritures exotiques en abondance, semblaient promettre une existence libérée des contraintes et des tensions créées par les communautés cultivées du monde occidental. Les récits d'aventures en Polynésie, en quête de l'« évasion », devinrent si populaires qu'en 1921, la maison d'édition G. P. Putnam's Sons publia une parodie de ces expéditions dans les mers du Sud, intitulée « The Cruise of the Kawa » (1921).

Bien qu'ouvertement satirique, ne serait-ce que par les photographies sélectionnées, le livre fut considéré comme authentique et son auteur invité à s'exprimer devant la National Geographic Society. Preuve fut ainsi donnée que la fiction était préférable à la réalité lorsqu'il s'agissait de traduire le paradis sur terre. Et c'est ainsi que naquit ce goût pour le fantasque qui allait imprégner le pop polynésien. Mais à l'origine, les récits rapportés de Polynésie touchaient un instinct bien plus archaïque.

« Sur l'île de Otaheite (Tahiti), où l'amour est la principale occupation, le luxe favori, ou, plus exactement, l'unique luxe des habitants, les corps et les âmes des femmes sont poussés à la perfection. » (Joseph Banks, 1743–1820, naturaliste embarqué à bord de l'Endeavour du Capitaine Cook).

Ce genre de remarques proférées par les premiers explorateurs firent de la jeune fille indigène nue, la vahiné, l'Eve du jardin d'Eden polynésien. Incarnant les promesses d'un amour sans limites, elle devint la première et principale icône du pop polynésien. Bientôt, le palmier, la hutte, la pirogue et toutes sortes de fleurs et d'animaux exotiques la rejoignirent dans la galerie des symboles populaires de la culture océanienne. Tant et si bien que le tiki ne fut plus qu'une figure parmi d'autres de la légendaire Polynesia Americana.

L'ukulele, fit son apparition lorsque se déchaîna l'engouement pour la musique hawaïenne dans les années 1920. Les musiciens hawaïens étaient invités après leurs prestations dans les boîtes de nuit, et les clubs eux-mêmes commencèrent à puiser dans le thème tropical. Les sols et les plafonds en bambou ou en rotin, les luxuriantes plantes tropicales et les peintures murales des îles servirent de décor aux citadins en quête d'évasion, leur donnant l'illusion de se trouver dans les mers du Sud.

Et bientôt l'imagination populaire se concentra sur une autre image. Même si les premiers zoos européens avaient commencé à montrer des « sauvages » vivants et si les journalistes se moquaient des dames de la bonne société qui se pâmaient en le voyant, la répulsion et l'attrait ressentis à la fois pour le « sauvage », son allure étrangement exotique, s'étaient inscrits dans les consciences civilisées des occidentaux. Dans le pop polynésien, cette fascination prit la forme de l'idole païenne Tiki.

TIKI : LOISIRS ET STYLE DE VIE D'UNE GENERATION

« Le système d'idolâtrie, qui prévalait chez un peuple séparé de la majorité de ses semblables par des océans infranchissables et possédant à un degré inhabituel des moyens non seulement de subsistance mais aussi de confort, est une démonstration navrante d'imbécillité, d'absurdité et de déchéance. » (Révérend William Ellis : *Polynesian Researches*, 1831)

Dans les années 1950, les Américains étaient prêts à récolter les bénéfices du dur labeur qui leur avait donné l'indépendance économique et l'abondance. Ils étaient sortis de la Seconde Guerre mondiale en héros et volaient sur un nuage de succès international et de reconnaissance. Mais la même éthique puritaine du travail qui les avaient conduits jusque-là, transportait avec elle tout un lot d'interdits sociaux et moraux qui restreignaient la libre jouissance de la prospérité.

Les soirées polynésiennes offrirent un exutoire à l'homme en complet de flanelle grise, elles lui permirent de régresser jusqu'à une naïveté primitive qui faisait fi des lois : s'exhiber en chemises aloha bariolées (pas besoin de les rentrer dans son pantalon), s'enivrer de doux breuvages exotiques aux noms évocateurs d'un idiome infantile (Lapu Lapu, Mauna Loa Puki), manger le cochon luau avec ses doigts, et se lancer dans des concours de houla et de limbo, permettait de lâcher la bride et de s'amuser au sein d'une société on ne peut plus conservatrice.

Une autre liberté offerte au « sauvage de banlieue » était de pouvoir contempler des photos de femmes indigènes aux seins nus, aussi longtemps que l'on restait dans le cadre de l'intérêt anthropologique, et de pratiquer ainsi une sorte d'érotisme de type National Geographic. Mais tandis que l'on allait quérir à nouveau la vahiné et toutes les autres icônes-clichés propres aux contrées mythiques des mers du Sud, une nouvelle figure de proue du pop polynésien fit son apparition : l'idole sculptée communément appelée tiki. Nonobstant le fait que le terme n'existe pas en langage hawaïen ou tahitien, et que les statues de pierre de l'île de Pâques étaient des moai et le sont restées, toutes les sculptures océaniennes devinrent pour le pop polynésien les membres d'une même famille heureuse : les tiki. Ces effigies primitives étaient un antidote au monde moderne du plastique et du chrome, des monuments élevés aux instincts primaires des hommes.

Bien qu'empruntant leur forme à leurs prédécesseurs polynésiens, les tiki américains étaient le plus souvent des interprétations libres de plusieurs styles insulaires assaisonnés d'une bonne dose de fantaisie de BD et d'objet d'art moderne. Même ceux que l'on aurait pu qualifier d' « authentiques » ne reproduisaient en

fait que quelques originaux ayant survécu à la « fureur iconoclaste » des missionnaires. Cette attitude libérale envers la contrefaçon avait commencé dans les îles hawaïennes lors des premiers contacts avec l'Occident, comme on peut le constater dans ce rapport de 1825 : « Les officiers du navire royal *Blonde*, lorsqu'ils résidèrent dans les îles, étaient particulièrement soucieux de se procurer quelques-unes des anciennes idoles pour les rapporter chez eux comme curiosités. La demande épuisa bientôt le stock disponible. Afin de vaincre la pénurie, les Hawaïens fabriquèrent des idoles et les noircirent à la fumée afin de leur conférer une apparence antique, et finalement réussirent leur supercherie. » (W. S. W. Ruschenberger : Extracts from the Journal of an American Naval Officer, 1841). Et plus d'un siècle après, le collectionneur d'art primitif Pablo Picasso, qui était un client avisé du marché aux puces, déclarait :
« On n'a pas besoin du chef-d'œuvre pour saisir l'idée. Le concept ou la caractéristique d'un style est entièrement accessible dans des exemples de second ordre et même dans des faux. » Par conséquent, les artistes américains, imprégnés de l'esprit du tiki, n'hésitèrent pas à recréer les têtes des dieux au gré de leur fantaisie.

Un parfait exemple de ce style est le tiki qu'Alec Yuill-Thornton dessina pour le bar *Tiki Bob* à San Francisco. Mi-George Jetson, mi-primitif moderne, cette sculpture avait peu de choses en commun avec les objets océaniens. Mais avec la signature tiki du *Luau* de Stephen Crane elle marque en réalité le commencement du style tiki. Pour la première fois, un tiki fut utilisé comme logo, fit office de gardien à l'entrée des établissements, fut dessiné sur le menu et sur les pochettes d'allumettes, et apparut sous forme de chopes, salières et poivrières.

Bob Bryant, surnommé « Sneaky » (le sournois), avait travaillé comme gérant du bar de Trader Vic, mais lorsque les deux hommes se brouillèrent en 1955, Bob quitta le *Trader* de Cosmo Place et ouvrit son propre bar. Sa tentative de vendre son concept au *Capitol Inn* de Sacramento fit long feu. Bob ouvrit également le *Tiki Bob's Mainland* sur la Bush Street où il offrit des défilés de lingerie pour attirer les hommes d'affaires à l'heure du déjeuner.

Tiki devint ainsi la star du théâtre pop polynésien, son nom étant adopté par une multitude d'établissements à travers l'Amérique, de l'Alabama à l'Alaska, ses différentes formes ornant les bars d'une civilisation fatiguée. L'image du tiki atteignit le sommet de sa popularité lorsqu'elle devint le logo de la série télé (produite par

Warner Brothers) « Hawaïan Eye » qui fut diffusée dans les foyers américains entre 1959 et 1963, sa forme archétypale marquant durablement les esprits des banlieusards hypnotisés.

Le grand conflit des générations des années 1960 mit un terme à la fièvre tiki alors que celle-ci était à son paroxysme. Les enfants des noceurs tiki décidèrent de créer leur Nirvana personnel, où l'amour libre et le bonheur loin du monde quotidien étaient une réalité immédiate. L'alcool cessa d'être la drogue de prédilection lorsque la marijuana et les psychotropes devinrent des substances récréatives, et que la révolution sexuelle parut mettre un terme au principe puritain de la monogamie. De même que la fausse cuisine pseudo-chinoise, trop grasse et trop sucrée, les cocktails tropicaux heurtaient la récente prise de conscience de l'alimentation saine.

L'« invasion anglaise » attira l'attention des jeunes vers un autre culte étranger bizarre, les Beatles. Les Kinks se lamentaient sur cette Polynésie en plastique : « … et même les pagnes étaient en PVC ! » Et de même que, deux siècles auparavant, les Polynésiens découvrirent que les explorateurs blancs n'étaient pas des dieux lorsque, à Kealakekua Bay, ils firent couler le sang du Capitaine Cook et le tuèrent, les Américains furent traumatisés lorsque leur divinité, le Président Kennedy, fut assassiné en 1963. Ce fut le commencement de la fin, la perte de leur innocence infantile, à leurs propres yeux et aux yeux du monde. La guerre du Viêt-nam se transformant dans les consciences en une monstrueuse erreur, avec ses huttes et ses palmiers brûlant sur les écrans de télé, l'exotisme et le style tiki se voyaient dénoncés comme des rituels imposés par l'establishment impérialiste. Et tandis que de jeunes manifestants marchaient sur le Capitole de Washington, Richard Nixon sirotait du Mai-Tai dans son repère favori, le Trader Vic's de Washington.

Dans les années 1970, le style polynésien ainsi discrédité fut noyé par l'apparition d'un thème tropical générique indéfini, sans identité claire, sans caractère insulaire. Qu'il s'agisse des Caraïbes, du Mexique ou de la Polynésie, partout on retrouvait « Margharita-ville ». Le show télévisé populaire « Fantasy Island » illustrait cette délimitation politiquement correcte de complicité culturelle, créant un monde au décor colonial en osier blanc mélangé à des plantes exotiques. Le bar habillé de fougères remplaça le bar tiki.

Les années 1980 furent la décennie de la destruction, de l'abolition du tiki et de sa culture. Rasés ou rénovés de manière à les rendre méconnaissables, les palaces polynésiens disparurent sans avoir été reconnus comme une facette unique de la culture pop américaine. Considérée comme l'expression d'une lubie populaire, ils avaient toujours été condamnés ou ignorés par les critiques de la culture et constituaient désormais une faute de goût embarrassante. Une tradition entière disparut sans qu'on le remarquât ni qu'on le déplorât.

ERIGER UN TEMPLE TIKI

La construction d'un « Hale Tik » (maison du tiki) était une entreprise complexe, non seulement à cause des différents matériaux exotiques employés, mais aussi en raison des concepts inhabituels utilisés pour étonner et enchanter les fidèles adorateurs du tiki tandis qu'ils ingurgitaient leurs breuvages tropicaux.

Ce chapitre donne un aperçu des motifs qui définissent, à l'intérieur comme à l'extérieur, l'architecture du style tiki, présentant ainsi un aspect de la culture pop américaine peu reconnu jusqu'ici. Bien qu'il existe une tradition distincte, instaurée par Don the Beachcomber et comportant des éléments sans cesse utilisés et améliorés, ce qui caractérise le style tiki c'est la façon dont chacun, saisi par la fièvre Tiki l'a recréé à sa façon. Des jungles artificielles aux rituels de présentation des cocktails, l'imagination s'emballait lorsque les promoteurs américains rêvaient à l'appel du tiki, donnant corps à leurs versions personnelles d'un sanctuaire des mers du Sud.

Le concept architectural favori était celui du pignon en A. Est-ce le fruit d'une coïncidence si, vers la fin des années 1950, le style néo-primitif tiki entra en concurrence avec son antithèse, le style futuriste de l'époque supersonique, ou bien l'un des deux était-il une réaction nécessaire à l'autre? Quoi qu'il en soit, les deux styles se rejoignaient glorieusement dans le pignon en A. Avec le terminal de la TWA de Eero Saarinen et la Première Eglise Unitarienne de Frank Lloyd Wright, les pignons s'élançant dans le ciel devinrent le jeu favori des architectes modernes, reflétant l'optimisme de l'âge de l'espace que l'on retrouvait aussi dans les ailerons des cadillacs.

Il se trouve que la majorité des habitations traditionnelles océaniennes étaient des huttes de palmier, et avaient nécessairement une forme en A. Mais comme les constructions polynésiennes, à l'exception des habitations sacrées maoris chargées de sculptures, étaient plutôt simples, d'autres groupes ethniques similaires furent mis à contribution. La maison cérémonielle de Nouvelle-Guinée, ou « haus

tambaran », avec son pignon allongé et son fronton orné de masques, et la maison cérémonielle des hommes de Paläu, Micrônésie, ornée de peintures narratives colorées, furent la source d'inspiration de nombreux temples tiki américains. Les enfants de l'âge du jet rencontraient ceux du silex lorsque les primitifs modernes garaient leurs voitures devant ces vaisseaux spatiaux de la planète tiki, franchissant sciemment le seuil d'un autre monde où ils pouvaient pour un moment devenir membres de la tribu tiki.

Les charpentes en A étaient faciles à construire, et des bâtiments traditionnels tels que les cabanes du Wisconsin ou des maisons de commerce furent transformés en palais païens par l'adjonction d'une entrée de forme pointue. Les restaurants chinois « actualisèrent » leur style, se donnant des allures de huttes pour bénéficier de la folie polynésienne. Mais que se passait-il derrière le grand A ? Afin de symboliser le seuil d'une autre réalité, il fallait souvent édifier un pont au-dessus d'un ruisseau alimenté par une cascade s'écoulant sur une paroi en pierre ponce. Le feu et l'eau entraient en scène avec des torches à gaz tiki, parfois fixées comme signaux lumineux au sommet des pignons, et des cascades intérieures et extérieures dont le doux murmure fournissait un fond sonore. Des tiki imposants flanquaient l'entrée, surgissant d'une jungle feuillue, et assuraient le rôle de colonnes de soutien. L'intérieur était un environnement complexe qui interpellait tous les sens. Les différentes salles, avec des noms aussi évocateurs que « Le Trou noir de Calcutta » ou « Le Bar des Sept Plaisirs », étaient recouvertes, du sol au plafond, de bois exotiques, de bambou, de rotin, mais aussi de tissu pour pagne, et d'autres matières organiques. Des armes primitives et des masques accrochés aux murs, des lampes-balises et divers objets suspendus au plafond formaient une partie du décor. Des peintures murales représentant des scènes de la vie dans les îles et des dioramas en trois dimensions renforçaient l'illusion de se trouver dans un pays lointain. La peau humaine était une autre texture essentielle. De nombreux établissements étaient fiers de leurs serveuses exotiques à peine vêtues, contrepartie vivante aux peintures sur velours noir qui étaient aussi un élément de décor commun à la plupart des bars tiki. Pour les guerriers en col blanc des années 1950, cela avait un charme particulier, qu'entretenaient les spectacles polynésiens devenus un divertissement standard dans beaucoup des clubs-restaurants des mers du Sud. Le fait que les danseurs de feu polynésiens et que

les danseuses de houlah tahitiennes fussent souvent d'origine sud-américaine ou asiatique était sans importance. Les costumes et la musique, les textures exotiques, le décor tropical et les puissants breuvages, tout contribuait à faire oublier les questions d'authenticité, ce qui permettait au noceur tiki de s'abandonner au charme irréel du paradis polynésien urbain.

Les diverses lampes, très originales, suspendues en rangs serrés à la plupart des plafonds des temples tiki, faisaient partie des objets artisanaux les plus curieux. Des pièges de pêcheur jetant une faible lumière, des boîtes en bois flotté, des cages à oiseaux, des tétrodons, des coquillages et des filets de pêche et leurs bouchons de liège formaient le ciel de la *Polynesia Americana*. Mais son habitant le plus imposant était toujours le tiki, saint patron du sauvage des banlieues.

DON THE BEACHCOMBER – LE PERE FONDATEUR DU POP POLYNESIEN

Hollywood, 1934 : la « noble expérimentation » américaine de la prohibition venait de s'achever. La demande en alcool de bonne qualité était importante, et un restaurateur émigré de la Nouvelle-Orléans, Ernest Beaumont-Gatt, décida de tenter sa chance avec le rhum. Peut-être inspiré par les histoires de pirates de sa ville natale, ou par le fait que son père, qui possédait un hôtel à la Nouvelle-Orléans, l'avait emmené à plusieurs reprises en Jamaïque, Ernest ouvrit un petit bar à McCadden Place, à Hollywood, le décora avec quelques faux palmiers et le baptisa *Don the Beachcomber* (Don, le batteur de grève). Là, il mélangeait l'or liquide tel un alchimiste à la recherche de la pierre philosophale, créant de puissants breuvages qui permettaient à ses clients de s'échapper temporairement vers les rivages lointains, tandis que dehors la vie de la grande ville suivait son cours effréné. Ernest s'identifia tellement à la figure du Beachcomber qu'il troqua légalement son nom contre celui de Don Beach. Bientôt sa science des mélanges attira la foule du cinéma assoiffée d'alcool et d'ambiance, et en 1937, il transforma son bouge en un repaire des mers du Sud qui allait devenir un modèle pour ceux qui suivirent ses traces. Telle une île dans l'océan urbain, Don fit de son paradis polynésien un refuge contre la métropole qui l'entourait.

L'aménagement intérieur était composé de matériaux exotiques tels que le bambou, des nattes en lahaula et des bois d'importation. Les plantes tropicales, des fleurs, des régimes de bananes et des noix de coco entretenaient l'atmosphère exotique, tandis que des armes indigènes et d'autres objets océaniens parlaient de civilisations sauvages. Des fragments d'épaves et d'objets venus des quatre coins du monde étaient suspendus au plafond, accentuant l'illusion d'être arrivé à un havre du plaisir. Une averse tombant sur le toit à intervalles réguliers et actionnée à la main donnait l'impression d'avoir échappé à un orage tropical, tandis qu'un flot de musique douce entraînait les habitués dans des rêveries exotiques. Le dépaysement était renforcé par l'effet des puissants cocktails imaginés par Don, parfois servis dans des ananas entiers ou lourdement décorés d'étranges garnitures. Mais si Don Beach possédait le sens du spectacle et une imagination fertile, il était peu doué pour les affaires. Cette partie du ressort de sa femme, Cora Irene « Sunny » Sund. Elle avait proposé un partenariat d'affaires qui avait abouti à un mariage en 1937, avant de se terminer par un divorce trois ans plus tard. Ce qui ne l'empêcha pas de conserver une emprise ferme sur la boutique, si ferme que lorsque Don revint de la guerre, à laquelle il avait pris part comme colonel de l'armée de l'air, il se vit dépossédé de son propre bar. Sunny, qui avait dirigé l'ouverture du premier franchisé à Chicago, en 1940, était désormais en charge de l'opération et n'avait plus besoin de Don, juste de son nom.

Beaucoup plus créateur qu'homme d'affaires, Don parvint à conserver une position de conseiller au *Don the Beachcomber* du continent, tout en consacrant toute son énergie à son projet chéri : ouvrir son propre local à Hawaii.

Mais Don avait également créé un prototype, le « beachcomber » urbain du XXᵉ siècle, un individu qui tenait à la fois du grand voyageur, du beatnik de plage et du noceur. Dans l'histoire du pop polynésien, d'autres « beachniks » firent leur apparition dont le plus notable fut Ely Hedley, également connu comme « le beachcomber original ».

Epicier malchanceux de l'Oklahoma, il avait suivi l'appel du Pacifique et entraîné sa famille à Whites Point, une plage située près de San Pedro à Los Angeles. Là-bas, lui, sa femme et leurs quatre filles se construisirent une maison en bois flotté et entamèrent un commerce fructueux en fabriquant des lampes et des meubles avec les épaves échouées à leur porte. Ely devint si célèbre pour son style « beachcomber moderne » qu'on lui confia la décoration de temples tiki tels que le *Trader Dick's* et le *Harvey* dans le Nevada. Lorsque la fièvre tiki se répandit, il commença à sculpter des tiki et à ouvrir des boutiques de produits des îles; d'abord à Huntington Beach, puis dans l'« Adventureland » de Disneyland. Après avoir définitivement apposé sa marque sur le style tiki, Edy Hedley se retira dans la résidence « Islander » de Santa Ana, décorée par ses soins.

Entre-temps, *Don the Beachcomber* était devenu un logo commercial, l'entreprise changeant deux fois de mains pour finalement appartenir à la société Getty. La figure avait été modernisée, troquant les traits de Don contre ceux d'un noceur anonyme. Les franchisés étaient maintenant au nombre de seize, certains comme les établissements de Dallas ou de Marina Del Rey ressemblant à des OVNIS. D'autres fans de la Polynésie s'inspirèrent, à travers les Etats-Unis, du concept Beachcomber, mais aucun n'avait le flair de Don. Lui-même s'était construit un nouveau royaume dans son Centre de Marché International à Waikiki. Là-bas, il continua à innover et à créer de « nouvelles façons de produire des choses » pour la Polynesia Americana. Lorsque Don disparut en 1987, les derniers établissements de la chaîne qui portait son nom, depuis longtemps abandonnés par son mana, mirent rapidement la clé sous la porte. Mais l'influence décisive de Don sur le phénomène du pop polynésien n'a pas été oubliée.

TRADER VIC – L'AMBASSADEUR DU BON GOUT

L'américanisation de tiki, en tant que dieu des loisirs, se fit progressivement. L'un de ses plus grands émissaires fut Victor Bergeron, plus connu sous le nom de Trader Vic, qui employa même ses propres figures mythologiques, les « Menehune » ou « petit peuple » des légendes polynésiennes. Ce n'était pas tant qu'il glorifiait ouvertement la divinité mais, malgré dans les années 50, le tiki était toujours avec lui, et Trader était devenu une figure plus grande que nature, un original, appartenant à une race en voie d'extinction, disparue aujourd'hui. A la fois patriarche, gentleman et phallocrate, son succès comme restaurateur et épicurien encouragea une génération de « sauvages cultivés », à tourner le dos à la civilisation et à créer leur Polynésie à eux dans les bars, les restaurants, les jardins, les arrière-cours et les bowlings. Il éleva « la bouffe et la bibine » des mers du Sud, comme il les appelait, au rang d'art. Plus encore que Don the Beachcomber, qui aurait dit-on trouvé le nom de son apéritif le « Rumaki » en laissant tomber son doigt sur une page d'un dictionnaire des îles Cook, Trader Vic fut un innovateur culinaire. Après le succès de sa cuisine « Nouveau Polynesian », il fut l'un des premiers à proposer des plats mexicains aux consommateurs américains (par le biais de ses restaurants Seor Pico).

Tout commença dans un bouge baptisé *Hinky Dinks*, à Oakland, de l'autre côté de la baie de San Francisco. Ce fut le premier établissement que Vic bâtit pour lui en 1934, une cabane de bois édifiée avec ses derniers 500 dollars. Dans l'histoire du pop polynésien, il y eut certains « centres de pouvoir », tels que le *Beachcomber* à Hollywood, le *Luau* à Beverly Hills, le *Lanai* à San Mateo ou le *Bali Hai* à San Diego, qui diffusaient le mana de Tiki. *Hinky Dinks*, qui allait bientôt devenir *Trader Vic's*, était l'un d'eux. Mais Victor Bergeron était un homme ambitieux, éminemment doué pour les cocktails étranges, et c'était exactement ce que les gens désiraient boire après l'abrogation de la prohibition. Il avait effectué un voyage d'études à Cuba et en Louisiane et étudié sa place avec les meilleurs barmen. Mais ce fut son séjour à Los Angeles qui s'avéra décisif. Dans sa biographie, il révèle :

« Nous sommes allés dans un établissement appelé *South Seas* qui n'existe plus, et nous avons même visité *Don the Beachcomber* à Hollywood. En fait, j'ai même fait des emplettes chez *Don the Beachcomber*. Lorsque je suis retourné à Oakland et que j'ai raconté à ma femme ce que j'avais vu, nous sommes tombés d'accord pour changer le nom et la décoration de notre restaurant. Nous avons décidé que *Hinky Dinks* était un nom à foutre en l'air et que l'endroit devait être baptisé du nom d'un personnage dont on pourrait raconter les histoires. Ma femme a suggéré *Trader Vic's* (Vic le marchand) parce que je faisais toujours du commerce avec mes clients. Parfait, je devins Trader Vic. » En conséquence de quoi, la jambe de bois qu'il avait gardée d'une lutte contre la tuberculose dans son enfance (et avec laquelle il divertissait ses clients en plantant parfois abruptement un pic d'acier) devint le fruit d'une rencontre avec un requin – l'un des nombreux contes correspondant à la nouvelle identité de Vic.

Cet aveu candide concernant la naissance de *Trader Vic* venait d'un homme qui avait non seulement égalé, mais dépassé son pair et prédécesseur. Vic n'eut jamais à dissimuler ses sources, parce qu'il ne perdit jamais le contrôle de son affaire comme Don, et lorsque la vogue polynésienne prit son essor dans les années 1950, il était en position d'en tirer le meilleur profit. Il ouvrit son premier poste avancé, qu'il appela *The Outrigger* à Seattle en 1949. Une flopée de clubs-restaurants satellites prit la suite au fil des décennies : à San Francisco proprement dit en 1951, à Denver en 1954, Beverly Hills 1955, Chicago 1957, New York et La Havane 1958, et Portland

1959. Ils furent suivis par d'autres à Boston, Houston, Dallas, Detroit, Atlanta, Kansas City, Saint Louis, Saint Petersbourg, Washington, Vancouver, Scottsdale, Londres, Munich et par une multitude d'établissements à l'étranger.

Vic élargit encore son influence avec une série de livres de recettes de cuisine et de cocktails, lesquels il utilisait de préférence des produits venant de sa nouvelle société Trader Vic's Food Products. Dans ces publications, il exposait ses vues sur les réunions et les habitudes alimentaires de la classe moyenne, et ce dans son argot caractéristique, bien différent de la prose fleurie qu'il utilisait dans ses menus :

« J'ai eu un tas d'emmerdes pour avoir déballé ce qui se passe quand on va chez quelqu'un pour bouloutter de la nourriture et se rincer le gosier, et je maintiens que la maîtresse de maison américaine moyenne a besoin d'une petite raclée dans son derrière culinaire, alors entrons dans le vif du sujet. C'est simple, les petits machins qu'on sert généralement dans les cocktails me tuent. Après avoir regardé pendant des années des centaines de plateaux en argent et leur contenu, j'en suis arrivé à la conclusion que quelqu'un aurait dû créer un prix Pulitzer pour le hors-d'œuvre le plus mortel. » Le Trader était un sacré fils de pute, et les gens l'aimaient pour ça.

Lorsque Hawaii devint la villégiature de rêve de l'Amérique, Vic fut contacté pour devenir le consultant culinaire d'United Airlines et des hôtels de la compagnie maritime Matson, les deux principales agences de voyages entre les îles et l'Amérique. Auparavant, autour de 1940, il avait monté un partenariat pour ouvrir un établissement à Honolulu, mais suite à un désaccord il y renonça, laissant à son partenaire le droit d'utiliser le nom dans les îles. Le fait étrange qu'un Trader Vic's ait été ouvert à Hawaii, comme Don the Beachcomber's, le Kon-Tiki de Stephen Crane et la Christian Hut avant lui, renforce la thèse selon laquelle le pop polynésien est véritablement une facette de la culture pop américaine, exportée à Hawaii pour répondre à l'attente des touristes.

Cette expansion de l'empire du Trader fut rendue possible grâce au soutien financier de grandes chaînes hôtelières, telles que Western (aujourd'hui Westin) et Conny Hilton, qui pouvaient s'offrir les constructions élaborées requises par un bar tiki de grande classe. Et de la classe, le Trader Vic's en avait à revendre. Si d'autres bars des mers du Sud, dont beaucoup avaient copié son nom, servaient les troufions, le Vic's était le club des officiers. Non que Vic fût snob, mais il voulait gagner rapidement de l'ar-

gent, et il y parvint en attirant les riches. Mais ce fut en définitive l'une des raisons de l'effondrement de la chaîne, car à mesure que disparaissaient les membres de la haute société fréquentant ces hauts lieux du plaisir, les nouvelles générations recherchaient des environnements plus abordables et moins chichiteux.

Les postes avancés de Seattle, Washington, Vancouver, Portland et même San Francisco ont malheureusement fermé leurs portes dans les années 1990. Mais Trader Vic's continue de bien se porter outre-mer et demeure la seule chaîne de bars tiki en Amérique. Ainsi, en dépit des malencontreux efforts de rénovation des années 1980, qui virent disparaître les lampes-cages à oiseaux caractéristiques, et d'autres éléments du décor considérés comme des nids à poussière, des havres hôteliers tels que le Trader Vic's de Chicago et celui de Munich restent les rares exemples du style tiki.

STEPHEN CRANE – L'HOMME QUI AIMAIT LES FEMMES

Dans la tradition polynésienne de Mangareva et des Marquises, tiki, le premier homme, est dépeint comme un filou et un charmeur. Après tout, c'est lui qui a créé la première femme avec de la boue, s'activant aussitôt après à faire avec elle tous les enfants de ce monde. Il paraît donc normal que celui qui reprit le flambeau tiki fût un homme de commerce agréable et un grand séducteur. Acteur raté de films de série B (« Le Cri du loup-garou »), le seul titre de gloire de Crane était d'avoir été marié à Lana Turner. Bien que cette union n'ait duré que cinq mois, une fille, Cheryl, en naquit. Bien plus tard, alors qu'elle était adolescente, celle-ci connut la célébrité en assassinant l'amant mafioso de Lana, Johnny Stompanato (apparemment parce qu'elle avait déjà été victime d'agressions sexuelles par un autre des soupirants de sa mère, le Tarzan de cinéma Lex Barker). Mais Stephen resta l'ami de Lana tout en séduisant d'autres stars. Le propriétaire du Ciro, le principal bar de Hollywood dans les années quarante, remarquait après avoir vu Steve trois soirs de suite avec successivement Ava Gardner, Rita Hayworth et Lana Turner : « Les trois plus grandes reines de cette ville ! Je n'ai jamais vu quelqu'un d'autre faire ça ».

Heureusement, l'énergie de Stephen Crane se concentra bientôt sur les mondanités et le divertissement. En 1953, il ouvrit son restaurant The Luau au 421 Rodeo Drive à Beverly Hills. L'endroit avait abrité auparavant le bar The Tropics, et Stephen broda sur le thème exotique dans l'intention de conserver la clientèle des gens du

cinéma. Il le fit à sa façon, comme s'en souvient sa fille Cheryl dans sa biographie « Detour: A Hollywood Story » : « Il considérait que puisque les hommes aiment traîner dans des endroits qui attirent les femmes, il fallait rendre le sien aussi appétissant qu'un pot de miel. Au centre du pot de papa, il y avait une stratégie peu connue, et jamais ébruitée : autoriser quelques prostituées triées sur le volet et très chères, à se mêler au reste de la clientèle du bar. Il s'agissait souvent d'ex-starlettes, elles étaient raffinées et magnifiquement vêtues, leur présence attirant les hommes sans choquer les autres femmes qui les reconnaissaient rarement pour ce qu'elles étaient. »

Et afin de tirer un profit maximum du principe de « La Belle et la Bête », Crane peu plus a paradis de tiki qu'il présentait ainsi dans son menu : « Les tiki, ces grandes sculptures délicieusement laides qui vous entourent doivent attirer votre attention. Un tiki est un géant, une idole. Alors qu'aujourd'hui la plupart de nos voisins des mers du Sud sont chrétiens, ils ne cessent de respecter et de vénérer les dieux de leurs ancêtres, et nous avons ici au Luau des tiki tels que le dieu de la pluie, le dieu du soleil, le dieu de la guerre et d'autres encore. Le tiki à la bouche exceptionnellement large est le dieu de la boisson, La Grande Gueule. Le tiki avec le plus gros bedon est notre préféré, peut-être parce qu'il est le dieu du bien manger ». Cette attitude pleine d'humour et naïve envers la religion éteinte d'un autre peuple caractériserait désormais le style tiki. Pour la première fois, un tiki inspiré des deux sculptures de l'entrée, était utilisé comme emblème sur le menu, les pochettes d'allumettes, les cartes postales, mais aussi comme pied de lampe en céramique ou comme salière et moulin à poivre.

Pour le reste du décor, Stephen s'était largement inspiré des traditions du Beachcomber et du Trader. Si largement, que le directeur artistique Florian Gabriel se souvient que pour un emploi de designer chez Stephane Crane and Associates, il lui fut impérativement demandé de se rendre au Trader Vic's du Beverly Hilton (qui jadis se vantait d'avoir à l'extérieur cinq tiki de 4,5 mètres de haut) et de faire un croquis d'un coin du restaurant. Il y parvint avec succès et à partir de ce moment, il forma une équipe de décorateurs avec George Nakashima, qui avait auparavant travaillé par Welton Becket, architecte du Beverly Hilton. Ils participèrent ensuite à la construction des îles satellites SCA qui commencèrent à s'implanter dans les autres villes américaines à la fin des années 1950.

La Sheraton Corporation, désireuse de rivaliser avec le *Hilton*, avait invité Crane à recréer d'abord son *Luau*, dans leur hôtel de Montréal, où il ouvrit sous le nom de *Kon-Tiki* en 1958, en présentant au public abasourdi « des panneaux de bois gravés par les Maoris avec des motifs particuliers pour se préserver des esprits malins, des lances de Nouvelle-Guinée avec des pointes en aile de chauve-souris trempées dans le poison par les chasseurs de têtes, et un autel pour les sacrifices ». Portland (avec trois cascades), Chicago, Dallas, Cleveland et Honolulu suivirent. Le *Kon-Tiki Ports* de Chicago et le *Ports of Call* de Dallas furent conçus selon le principe du touriste voyageant dans son fauteuil et donnèrent à chaque salle à manger un thème différent : Papeete, Singapour, Macao et Saïgon. Leurs histoires étaient de la pure poésie pop polynésienne : « PAPEETE – Un des quatre points d'ancrage exotiques à Ports o' Call Restaurant dans le penthouse du Southland Center, Dallas, Texas. La nature a été domptée pour ce refuge tropical. Une cascade murmure pour votre plaisir et les animaux sauvages ne bougent pas, pour que vous vous sentiez à l'aise. Mais les lances et les peaux de bêtes rappellent au convive que la vie simple a ses côtés excitants. »

Quoi qu'il en soit, le fossé que la réalité allait bientôt creuser entre la génération tiki et ses enfants manifestant contre la guerre du Viêt-nam n'est nulle part mieux illustré que dans la description du salon SAIGON : « La splendeur orientale et l'opulence marquent ce Port du Plaisir. Ces heureux habitants sont entourés de feuilles d'or fin, de soies rares, de cristal et de sculptures de temples autrefois interdits. » Ce qui était une licence poétique en 1960 était douloureusement cynique vers 1968. A la fin des années 1970, un consortium iranien offrit à Stephen Crane 4,1 millions de dollars pour le *Luau*. En 1979, l'établissement fut totalement rasé : la fin de l'ère tiki s'annonçait.

DANNY BALSZ – LE FILS PRODIGUE

La figure de Danny Balsz ne s'inscrit pas naturellement dans la lignée des ancêtres du pop polynésien. Il ne lança pas de chaîne de restaurants et n'imposa pas non plus d'innovations culinaires ou de nouveaux breuvages alcoolisés. Il n'était pas tant concerné par la qualité que par la quantité. Pour Danny Balsz, plus c'était gros et mieux c'était. Par conséquent, il construisit le plus gros volcan sur le terrain du plus grand luau polynésien de ce pays. Là-bas, chaque nuit, une jeune fille tiki était jetée en sacrifice dans cette fosse ardente, tandis que des danseurs tahitiens, dans des costumes qui devaient plus au Las Vegas

de l'époque qu'à la réalité insulaire, se trémoussaient aux rythmes de divers orchestres. Lorsqu'il découvrit que les Hawaïens étaient censés croire que plus on avait de tiki dans sa demeure et plus on avait de chance, il s'entoura de poteaux figuratifs en bois de toutes formes et dimensions, et baptisa l'endroit *The Tikis*. Plus de dieux, plus de danseurs, plus de nourriture et de boisson pour plus de 3 000 clients chaque nuit. C'était un tiki pour les masses, et Danny était Mr.Tiki !

The Tikis incarne l'apogée de l'ère tiki. Il s'éleva avec une grandeur et une décadence sans précédent avant de disparaître dans l'oubli. En butant contre les ruines de ce Disneyland des dieux oubliés, je sus que son histoire serait un jour racontée. Devant moi s'étendait la planète perdue des tiki, le cimetière des éléphants d'une espèce disparue. Qu'est-ce qui avait conduit cette civilisation autrefois grandiose au déclin ? Fils d'un propriétaire de night-clubs de la ville frontière de Mexicali, Danny Balsz émigra à l'est de Los Angeles, avec en tête le souvenir de plaisirs incertains. Travaillant dix ans comme boucher d'abattoir, jusqu'au jour où il opta pour l'aménagement paysager et se spécialisa dans les cascades. Un jour de 1958, Danny fit des emplettes chez un pépiniériste japonais à Monterey Park, un faubourg rural de Los Angeles coincé entre quatre autoroutes. En s'arrêtant à un ranch voisin pour y acheter des œufs, il fit la connaissance de sa propriétaire, Doris Samson. Quatre mois plus tard, ils étaient mariés. Tout en aidant Doris avec ses poulets, Danny peaufinait ses talents de paysagiste, transformant lentement le dixième d'hectare de la propriété en un jardin tropical. En 1960, deux étudiants demandèrent à Danny s'ils pouvaient organiser une soirée luau sur le terrain. A cette époque, les terrains de luau, qu'on louait pour des soirées, surgissaient partout dans le sud du pays. Danny et Doris décidèrent de tuer tous leurs poulets et de se lancer dans le commerce des soirées polynésiennes. Le moment était bien choisi, l'endroit prospéra, et année après année, Danny versait et sculptait de plus en plus de ciment pour créer des tunnels de lave, des grottes et des chutes d'eau, édifiant de ses mains son propre Xanadu.

A la fin des années 1960, sa clientèle, essentiellement composée de travailleurs des sociétés d'aéronautique et de transport routier, débarquait par bus entiers. Les fournitures nécessaires, comme 50 000 guirlandes de l'usine de fleurs en plastique de Hughestown, Pennsylvanie et des tonnes d'ananas, étaient payées cash, et lorsqu'il restait de l'argent, Danny rap-

portait de nouveaux tiki. « J'avais tout, mec : l'argent, les voitures, les bagues ! », se souvenait Danny. Mais il voulait davantage. La chance de Danny tourna quand il commit le Péché de chair et il fut chassé du paradis pour être tombé amoureux de Leilani, une Hawaïenne mormon qui dansait dans l'établissement *The Tikis*. Les dieux ne virent pas d'un bon œil l'union du haolé et de la vahiné. Encore moins sa femme et ses enfants, qui constituaient l'épine dorsale de son opération familiale. Et sous la pression de voisins excédés, le conseil municipal lui retira sa licence. C'en était fini du cirque polynésien, semble-t-il. Mais Danny Balsz était monté sur des ressorts. Il remballa ses tiki et leur construisit un nouveau logis à Lake Elsinore, plus loin au sud de Los Angeles. Là, il trima pendant des années, reconstruisant un nouveau pays de lave. Ses tiki montaient patiemment la garde à l'entrée, attendant la grande réouverture. Mais les temps avaient changé et le grand jour ne vint jamais.

« La lumière qui brûle deux fois avec le même éclat, brûle deux fois moins longtemps, et tu as brûlé avec tant et tant d'éclat. Tu est le fils prodigue ! – Mais j'ai accompli des choses discutables … Et aussi des choses extraordinaires, tu as pleinement joui de ton temps… » (Extrait du dialogue du film « Bladerunner » de Ridley Scott)

KON-TIKI, AKU AKU ET THOR

« Les mystères non résolus des mers du Sud m'avaient fasciné. Il doit bien y avoir une solution rationnelle, me disais-je, et je m'étais promis d'identifier Tiki, le héros légendaire. »

Ainsi s'exprimait en 1937 un jeune zoologiste norvégien nommé Thor Heyerdahl, alors qu'il luttait pour survivre à Fatu Hiva, une des îles Marquises. Hippies avant l'heure, Thor et Liv avaient décidé de renoncer à la civilisation et de « retourner à la nature », vivant comme des primitifs en menant des recherches sur la faune locale pour le compte de l'Université d'Oslo. Mais lorsque Thor entendit Tei Tetua, le dernier natif à avoir goûté la chair du « Grand cochon » (l'homme), réciter un vieux conte le soir au coin du feu, tout bascula. « Tiki était à la fois un dieu et un chef. Ce fut Tiki qui amena nos ancêtres sur ces îles où nous vivons. Avant cela, nous vivions sur une grande terre, très loin, de l'autre côté de la mer. »

Dès lors, Thor cessa d'observer les escargots et les mille-pattes géants vénéneux, pour s'intéresser aux origines de la race polynésienne. Il avait été frappé par les similitudes entre les tiki de pierre, les pétroglyphes des Marquises, et les idoles incas

183

du Pérou ; et pendant dix ans, il travailla sur la théorie selon laquelle le grand prêtre pré-Inca, et fils du soleil, Kon-Ticï Viracocha, qu'un chef de guerre avait contraint à fuir le Pérou, ne faisait qu'un avec Tiki, le dieu ancestral polynésien. Ne rencontrant que résistance et mépris de la part des archéologues, des ethnologues, des linguistes et des sociologues, Thor résolut de prouver sa théorie par la pratique. Il construisit un radeau précolombien avec cabine en balsa, sans utiliser la moindre pointe, clou ou fil de fer, et se laissa dériver avec cinq hommes d'équipage scandinaves dans le détroit de Humboldt du Pérou à la Polynésie.

Après seulement trois mois de traversée, le Kon-Tiki parvint à rallier les côtes polynésiennes. Le livre inspiré par ce voyage, intitulé « L'Expédition du Kon-Tiki » fut publié pour la première fois en Norvège en 1948, et la critique l'accueillit fraîchement, comparant la tentative à « une descente des chutes du Niagara dans un tonneau ». Mais cela ne parvint pas à détourner l'intérêt du public pour cette entreprise intrépide.

Peu après la publication du livre en Angleterre et aux Etats-Unis, en 1950, il apparut évident que les éditeurs tenaient là un best-seller. « Kon-Tiki » fut finalement traduit en soixante langues, le premier livre après la Bible à connaître pareille diffusion. Le film réalisé au cours du voyage connut un destin similaire, après avoir été refusé par les distributeurs américains en raison de ses défauts techniques. Il reçut l'Academy Award du meilleur documentaire en 1951, et des millions de spectateurs allèrent le voir. Le monde sortait du traumatisme de la Deuxième Guerre mondiale et des aventures pacifiques étaient les bienvenues.

L'engouement international sans précédent pour le Kon-Tiki alimenta la fascination de l'Amérique pour la culture polynésienne. Bien que le terme « style tiki » n'ait pas été courant dans les années 1950 et 1960, il devint alors une expression populaire pour désigner l'architecture polynésienne. Thor et Tiki, le dieu nordique de la foudre et le dieu polynésien du soleil, s'étaient unis pour devenir des héros populaires. Le livre de Heyerdahl « Aku Aku » (1955), consacré à son expédition sur l'île de Pâques, eut également une grande influence sur la pop polynésien. La couverture du livre avait une icône si populaire que les gigantesques statues de pierres, les moaï, devinrent célèbres sous le nom de têtes Aku Aku, voire même de Aku-Tiki, et un thème largement répandu dans le royaume tiki américain.

JAMES MICHENER ET BALI HAI

« Bali Hai peut t'appeler, et la nuit. et le jour.
Dans ton cœur tu l'entendras, viens ici, viens ici.
Bali Hai murmurera, dans le vent, dans la mer,
Me voici, ton île à toi, viens vers moi, viens vers moi. Tous tes espoirs, tous tes rêves, fleurissent sur la colline, et brillent dans le courant. Si tu essaies, tu me trouveras, là où le ciel rencontre la mer, me voici, je suis à toi, viens vers moi, viens vers moi. » (d'après « South Pacific » de Rodgers et Hammerstein).
Thor ne fut pas le seul auteur à succès à marquer le pop polynésien de son empreinte. Au cours de la Deuxième Guerre mondiale, toute une génération de conscrits américains avait découvert la culture des îles du Pacifique. James Michener était l'un d'eux, et son récit onisoré de leur expérience, « Contes du Pacifique Sud », lui valut le Prix Pulitzer en 1948 et un extraordinaire succès populaire. Une comédie musicale de Broadway et un film en CinémaScope réussirent si bien à conférer un tour romantique aux épreuves de la guerre qu'ils donnèrent naissance à un nouveau terme pour désigner le « paradis exotique » : « Bali Ha'i », l'île des femmes. Il devint le nouveau Shangri-La, l'île de rêve de chaque homme.

C'est là-bas que le héros du roman, le Lieutenant Cable, fit l'expérience de ce vieux fantasme masculin d'un amour sans entraves une jeune beauté exotique. Le protagoniste de l'histoire se voit accorder le privilège de visiter l'île, « un joyau sur le vaste océan », sur lequel « les Français, avec une prévoyance et une connaissance toute gauloise de ces choses, avaient rassemblé toutes les femmes des îles. Chaque femme, qu'importe sa couleur ou son physique, qui aurait sinon été violée par les Américains, fut cachée à Bali Ha'i. » (Michener)
Lorsque le bateau du Lieutenant Cable jette l'ancre, les lecteurs masculins de 1950 ne peuvent que l'envier : « Pour la première fois de sa vie, il avait vu tant de femmes, en vérité toutes les femmes, aller et venir sans le moindre vêtement ... comme la jungle, comme les fruits de la jungle, les adolescentes semblaient se trouver là en une invraisemblable profusion. » (Michener)
Cable est sauvé de cet essaim de jeunes femmes par la matrone Bloody Mary qui le précipite immédiatement dans les bras de sa ravissante fille vierge Liat. Dans le film, le héros pénètre dans une romantique hutte en feuilles de palmier, où l'attend Liat, une fille ravissante et prête à l'amour.

Aucune parole n'est échangée, des regards brûlants, des lèvres tremblantes, l'amour est immédiat et profond. Les archétypes des mers du Sud doivent être vrais après tout.

Les Américains de toutes extractions firent soudain la connaissance d'une culture totalement étrangère grâce à un témoin direct, et cela laissa une marque indélébile sur l'Amérique elle-même : « Qu'est-ce que je fais là ? Comment moi, Joe Cable de Philadelphie, en suis-je arrivé là ? Voici Bali Ha'i, et il y a un an je n'en avais jamais entendu parler. Qu'est-ce que je fais là ? » (Michener). L'attitude était celle d'un émerveillement juvénile, et parce que les soldats avaient reçu un accueil chaleureux des populations libérées de l'envahisseur nippon, les souvenirs des années de service dans le Pacifique Sud étaient généralement excitants ou agréables. Par conséquent, de petites Bali Hai surgirent partout aux Etats-Unis, accueillant ceux qui y étaient allés aussi bien que ceux qui étaient restés. James Michener connut un nouveau succès avec « Retour au paradis » en 1951. Par la suite, il publia « Canailles au Paradis » (1957, avec un récit de la vie d'Edgar Leeteg) et « Hawaii » (1959) qui firent définitivement de lui l'auteur sur la Polynésie le plus lu dans les années 1950.
Michener avait visité la véritable Bali Ha'i, sur l'îlot de Mono, près de Guadalcanal. Il s'en souvenait comme d'un « village sale et désagréable », mais il se servit de son nom à cause de « sa qualité musicale ». Cela n'empêcha pas le mythe pop polynésien de Bali Hai d'être finalement réimporté en Polynésie française. En 1961, gravement atteints par la fièvre tiki, un avocat, un agent de changes et un vendeur d'articles de sport décidèrent de renoncer à leur existence civilisée à Newport Beach, dans la banlieue de Los Angeles, pour s'établir à Tahiti. Là-bas, ils ouvrirent un hôtel qu'ils baptisèrent naturellement « Bali Hai ». La fiction était devenue réalité, comme si souvent dans la pop polynésien.

LES EXPERTS EN MELANGES ET LEURS BREUVAGES par Jeff Berry

Quel restaurant oserait baptiser des fruits au sirop déposés sur un tas de fromage blanc « Les Ports du Désir » ? Le Luau le pouvait – essentiellement parce qu'on y servait les meilleurs cocktails exotiques au rhum de Beverly Hills. De tels breuvages étaient le carburant qui faisait tourner les roues du commerce des restaurateurs polynésiens. Plus que de simples cocktails, ils furent dès le début présentés comme des fantaisies en technicolor qui s'adressaient autant à l'œil qu'au palais, servis avec des garnitures originales dans des récipients qui s'étaient plus encore. Même la glace qui les accompagnait était sculptée dans des formes inusitées, moulée en cylindre autour de votre paille, ou en forme d'igloo afin que votre boisson vous arrive « endormie dans une grotte de glace ». Un drink pouvait aussi bien arriver fumant, flambant, ou garni d'un gardénia flottant dans lequel une perle dissimulée attendait d'être découverte.

Le cocktail était le principal sujet de conversation. En quittant un restaurant polynésien, on ne parlait pas de la nourriture – on parlait de la « Mystérieuse boisson », du « Penang Afrididi », ou du « Bouquet de feu Pelé ». Et les serveurs commençaient généralement par présenter la carte avec laquelle les descriptions poétiques accompagnaient des illustrations en couleur, quasiment hyperréalistes, des cocktails. Comme disait The Islander à propos de son Mont Kilauea : « Une éruption des rhums les plus subtils enflammés par les nectars sacrés des dieux tiki. »

Comme on pouvait s'y attendre, ces mélanges n'étaient pas toujours aussi bons qu'ils étaient beaux. Mais les meilleurs cocktails tropicaux pouvaient être complexes et à plusieurs niveaux ; d'abord subtils et voluptueux, avec un équilibre délicat entre douceur et amertume, puis forts et légers, fruités et secs. Et on trouvait les meilleurs cocktails tropicaux chez Don the Beachcomber's.

Lorsque Don ouvrit son premier bar en 1934, le rhum n'avait pas bonne réputation. D'ailleurs les alcooliques étaient appelés des « rummies ». Seuls les marins et les durs à cuire buvaient du tafia ; les gens élégants buvaient du whisky et du gin. Et si Don n'a pas inventé de cocktails à base de whisky et de gin, c'est pour la simple raison que le rhum était moins cher. Lorsque la prohibition s'acheva, on pouvait en acheter des caisses pour à peine 70 cents le litre. Dans le cas de Don, le sens de l'économie fut le moteur de l'invention. Mais non seulement Don ne créa ses « Rum Rhapsodies » à partir de rien. Nash Aranas, autrefois superviseur et « garant d'authenticité » de la chaîne de restaurants du Beachcomber, raconta en 1989 que Don avait « séjourné aux Antilles où lui était venue l'idée du rhum ». Don avait probablement découvert le Planter's Punch jamaïcain et le Daïquiri cubain ; ces deux boissons sont un simple mélange de citron vert, de sucre et de rhum – trois ingrédients qui devinrent la base de la plupart des créations de Don. Au citron vert, il ajouta l'ananas, la papaye et le fruit de la passion ; au sucre, il ajouta l'anis, la vanille

et l'extrait d'amande ; au rhum, il ajouta les liqueurs, des brandies parfumés ... et puis du rhum et encore du rhum. Don avait en effet découvert que mélanger des rhums bruns avec des rhums blancs créait des saveurs de base inédites, plus complexes, pour relever ses jus et ses sirops. « Don pouvait rester assis toute la journée avec ses copains à mélanger des ingrédients », se souvient Aranas. « Il testait, testait, testait, testait, comme un savant fou. » Les combinaisons étaient sans fin et variaient à l'infini, aboutissant à des inventions aussi populaires que le Vicious Virgin, le Shark's Tooth, le Cobra's Fang, le Dr.Funk et le Missionary's Downfall :

La légende veut que le zombie cocktail de Don, le Zombie, ait été improvisé afin de permettre à un client ayant la gueule de bois de participer à un rendez-vous d'affaires. Quand on lui demanda comment le remède avait agi, le client répondit : « Je me suis senti comme un mort-vivant – ça m'a transformé en zombie. » Mais la copie d'un menu du Beachcomber de 1941 propose une autre origine à ce cocktail : « Le Zombie n'est pas venu comme ça. C'est le résultat d'un long et coûteux processus. Au cours des expérimentations qui ont conduit au Zombie, le contenus de trois caisses et demie de différents rhums ont été utilisés et ont fini dans l'évier pour que vous puissiez aujourd'hui apprécier ce puissant ‹raccommodeur de rêves brisés›. »

Peu de temps avant sa mort, le barman et vétéran, Ray Buhen, l'un des employés du Beachcomber en 1934, donna une autre version de l'histoire. « Don était un chic type », se souvenait Buhen, qui avait ouvert son propre bar, le Tiki Ti, vingt-sept ans après. « Mais il s'écoutait parler. Il prétendait avoir inventé le Zombie, mais c'est faux. Et il n'a inventé pratiquement aucun de ses cocktails. » Buhen soutenait que le plus gros de ce travail fut accompli par les « Quatre gars », un quatuor d'assistants philippins de Don qui travaillaient derrière le bar. Une affirmation hérétique, c'est certain, mais la crédibilité de Ray ne peut être mise en cause. Durant soixante-deux années, il fut expert en mélanges dans les plus célèbres palaces polynésiens, du Seven Seas et du Luau au China Trader et à son propre bar, servant à boire à des gens tels que Clark Gable, Charlie Chaplin, Buster Keaton, les Marx Brothers et Marlon Brando.

Quelles que soient leurs origines, les cocktails de Don devinrent si rapidement populaires que les « Quatre gars » furent bientôt débordés. Don dut finalement recruter sept barmen à plein temps, chacun d'eux étant spécialisé dans différents cocktails.

Derrière eux, il y avait encore plus d'assistants philippins découpant les ananas avec des fils d'acier, taillant de gros blocs de glace jusqu'à en avoir mal aux bras et pressant des citrons verts jusqu'à ce que l'acide leur rongeait les ongles. Pour ajouter l'humiliation à la souffrance, la sécurité fut renforcée afin qu'aucun de ces assistants ne pût mémoriser les recettes secrètes de Don. Au lieu d'étiquettes, les bouteilles étaient identifiées par des chiffres et des lettres. Selon un article paru en 1948 dans le Saturday Evening Post : « Les recettes sont codées et les barmen suivent une liste de symboles qui indiquent les ingrédients pré-mélangés, plutôt que les véritables noms des concentrés de fruits et des différents rhums. De cette façon, même si un restaurateur rival parvenait à débaucher un membre de l'équipe du Beachcomber... le renégat ne pourrait pas emporter avec lui les recettes de Don. »

Néanmoins, cette recette du Zombie fut publiée dès 1941 :

Si Don était le Grand Patriarche Blanc du cocktail tropical, il eut de nombreux fils prodigues. Les imitations apparurent pratiquement aussitôt après l'ouverture de son établissement. Au night-club Tropics de Harry Sugerman, à Beverly Hills, le Zombie devint le Zoulou : « Un verre et vous êtes important ! Deux verres et vous êtes impatient ! Trois verres et vous êtes impuissant ! » Mais tandis que les autres se contentaient d'imiter Don, Trader Vic avait plus d'ambition. « Je ne connaissais rien à ce type de boissons », écrivit-il dans son autobiographie, « et j'ai pensé que j'aimerais apprendre. » Il voyagea un peu partout, observant des experts en mélanges de renommée mondiale comme Constantine Ribailagua à La Havane (qui créa le Papa Dobles Grapefuit-Daiquiri pour Hemingway) et Albert Martin de la Nouvelle-Orléans (connu pour son Ramos Fizz). Lorsqu'il revint à son saloon d'Oakland, Trader Vic avait cessé d'être un imitateur. Il était devenu un innovateur.

Lorsque Vic créa le Scorpion, le Samoan Fog Cutter et le Mai Tai, il devint soudain celui que tout le monde imitait. « Ceci aggrave sérieusement mon ulcère », pestait-il, lorsque les bars de Tahiti à Tulsa commençaient à s'approprier l'invention du Mai Tai. « Quiconque prétend que je n'ai pas créé ce cocktail », déclarait Vic, « est un fichu salaud. » Il raconta l'invention avec sa modestie habituelle : « J'étais derrière mon bar un jour de 1944, bavardant avec mon barman, et je lui dis que j'allais faire le meilleur cocktail au rhum du monde. C'est alors qu'entrèrent Ham et Carrie Guild, de vieux amis de Tahiti. Carrie y goûta, leva son verre, et prononça ces mots : « Mai Tai – Roa Ae » ce qui en tahitien signifie « D'un autre monde ! – le meilleur ! » C'est le nom du cocktail, ai-je dit, et nous l'avons baptisé Mai Tai » Voici la recette du Vic.

La controverse sur le véritable inventeur du Mai Tai ne prit fin qu'en 1970, lorsque Trader Vic porta l'affaire devant les tribunaux et traîna en justice la Sun-Vac Corporation. A cette époque, celle-ci exploitait la licence d'une gamme de cocktails pré-préparés sous le nom de Don The Beachcomber. Ironie du sort, Sun-Vac prétendait que c'était Don lui-même – l'homme que Vic admettait avoir pillé trente ans auparavant – qui avait inventé le Mai Tai. Le tribunal donna finalement raison à Vic. Lorsque les cocktails exotiques au rhum devinrent une grosse industrie et que les palaces polynésiens prospérèrent en les servant à leurs clients, la compétition se fit encore plus féroce. Contrairement à Don et Vic, les nouveaux venus ne pouvaient se réclamer d'aucune renommée, ils cherchèrent donc à se donner une légitimité en créant leurs propres barmen célèbres – souvent en faisant participer les membres du personnel à des concours de cocktails financés par des marques de rhum. Le restaurant pouvait ensuite faire sa publicité sur son propre cocktail créé par son propre barman légendaire, et la marque de rhum annoncer que la recette gagnante était réalisée avec leur rhum. En 1953, un serveur inconnu du Luau, du nom de Popo Galcini, fut engagé dans une compétition de ce type sponsorisée par Ron Rico. Il fut déclaré vainqueur et acquit ainsi une gloire instantanée, en dépit des rumeurs selon lesquelles, cette compétition, comme la plupart de ce genre, était truquée. Quoi qu'il en soit, Galcini fut vite débauché du Luau par le célèbre Kelbo's, dans l'ouest de Los Angeles, où il entama la première d'une série lucrative d'emplois de barman, qui atteignit son apogée à l'Outrigger à Laguna Beach. La carte des boissons du Outrigger annonçait fièrement « Cocktails Primés par POPO ». L'un de ceux-ci était le Pikake qui obtint le premier prix lors d'un concours en 1958.

Les cocktails « primés » n'étaient pas la seule façon de se distinguer pour les bars tiki. Si on ne pouvait en revendiquer l'invention, il restait toujours l'expertise. N'étant plus méprisé, le rhum était largement répandu au milieu des années 1950, et ce en particulier grâce au prosélytisme de Vic et de Don, qui commencèrent à fabriquer leurs propres mélanges et à vendre leurs propres marques. La bonne société renonça à son whisky et à son gin pour le rhum démoniaque, désormais teinté de romantisme comme le breuvage des « aventuriers des mers » et « la boisson la plus fabuleuse et la plus discutée de tous les temps » (du moins selon le Hawaiian Room à Omaha, Nebraska). Les épicuriens gravitaient autour des palais polynésiens possédant le plus grand assortiment de rhums rares, vieux, ou tout autre signe distinctif. Les restaurateurs annonçaient leurs « caves à rhum » ou exhibaient leurs vastes assortiments derrière le bar. Au sommet de la splendeur, Don the Beachcomber's proposait 120 différentes sortes de rhum. Certains établissements annonçaient pas seulement une très large assortiment de rhums, mais aussi de cocktails à base de rhum. « Vous trouverez un choix de 36 cocktails tropicaux », rapportait une chronique gastronomique du China Trader à Burbank, « et un professeur de Cal Tech a établi un record en réussissant à en ingurgiter seize avant de sombrer dans la béatitude. » Espérons du moins que ce professeur ne s'est jamais rendu au Luau qui n'affichait pas moins de 74 cocktails exotiques – y compris le Martiki, la « réponse polynésienne au Martini dry ».

Dans les années 1960, même les plus brillants intellectuels se rassemblaient dans les bars tiki. Les cinéastes Bob Fosse et Stanley Kubrick étaient tous deux des habitués du Trader Vic's de New York. C'est là qu'en 1964, Kubrick annonça pour la première fois l'idée qui, quatre ans plus tard, deviendrait 2001 : L'Odyssée de l'espace. On ignore ce qu'il buvait ce soir-là mais il pouvait sans doute en remontrer au professeur de Cal-Tech. Dans son autobiographie, Gore Vidal se souvient d'avoir emmené au Luau l'éminent historien Arthur Schlesinger et le Prix Nobel d'Economie John Kenneth Galbraith et, tous deux « imbibés de rhum », d'avoir brisé avec leurs plusieurs barreaux du gouvernail géant de l'entrée, en hurlant : « C'est le navire de l'Etat ! ». Frank Sinatra était un grand amateur du Navy Grog que l'on servait au Don The Beachcomber's de Palm Springs. Il laissait de généreux pourboires, se souvient le barman Tony Ramos, « mais il criait et vociférait s'il n'était pas servi assez rapidement. »

A l'aube des années 1970, les goûts commencèrent à changer. Le Missionary's Downfall céda la place au Screaming Orgasm, et les maîtres mélangeurs de l'Age d'or se dispersèrent aux quatre vents : emportant avec eux leur savoir, leur expérience et leurs « ingrédients secrets ». Demandez aux barmen d'aujourd'hui de vous confectionner un cocktail tropical, et le résultat écœurant donnera tristement raison à Tony Ramos qui affirme que le mélange des cocktails exotiques est un « art disparu ».

Néanmoins, comme en témoigne ce livre, il existe encore une poignée d'endroits qui offrent de vrais cocktails exotiques. Le Mai Kai à Fort Lauderdale, Floride, et le Kahiki à Columbus, Ohio, continuent de servir des Breuvages Mystérieux dans des coupes fumantes, présentées par de jeunes indigènes peu vêtues, au son des gongs rituels. Et le Tiki Ti du défunt Ray Buhen, aujourd'hui dirigé par son fils Mike, continue de servir 72 cocktails exotiques aux habitants de Los Angeles.

Quelle meilleure façon de conclure ce chapitre sur l'histoire des boissons américaines que de citer les paroles de Ray : « C'est de l'évasion. C'est irréel. C'est du bidon », déclarait-il au sujet des faux cocktails polynésiens. Et il ajoutait : « Ah, c'était le bon temps. »

… ET LES DIEUX FURENT DIVERTIS

Hawaii, 1820, c'est la fête. Observant les indigènes en train d'offrir des leis (guirlandes de fleurs) à une idole au cours d'un marathon de houla, le missionnaire Hiram Bingham s'efforce de comprendre. « Quelle est la fonction de votre dieu, à quoi est-il bon ? » Leur réponse simple l'intrigue : « A jouer ! » Ce qui était alors inconcevable pour le puritain, les Américains seraient aptes à le comprendre un peu plus d'un siècle plus tard. Leur droiture et leur modestie leur avaient permis de surmonter la dépression et les avaient aidés à gagner la Seconde Guerre mondiale. La sécurité économique paraissait accordée à chacun et le temps était venu de jouer. Mais il n'était pas facile de mettre au panier la morale inébranlable des aïeux qui réfrénait ses désirs. Il fallut créer un autre monde où l'on pourrait assumer une personnalité moins restreinte. La culture apparemment insouciante de la Polynésie devint un univers parallèle pour ceux qui étaient en mal d'évasion. Là où l'on pouvait s'amuser, tiki régnait.

Vu la multitude d'idées mises en pratique pour distraire les clients, les bars tiki étaient déjà devenus de véritables petits parcs d'attractions. Y réunir des temples tiki ou créer des parcs tiki était donc dans l'ordre des choses. La Californie et la Floride, lieux de villégiature par excellence, offraient une parfaite combinaison de personnes en quête de loisirs et de climat doux, et l'on vit surgir des univers tiki tels que Tiki Gardens et The Tikis. Naturellement, le Grand Kahuna des parcs d'attractions, Walt Disney en personne, ne fut pas en reste. Client assidu des clubs-restaurants polynésiens, il décida de créer un restaurant tiki qui surpasserait tous les autres. Walt était un animateur, et pour lui l'étape suivante fut logiquement de donner vie au décor habituel : fleurs, oiseaux et tiki. Ce fut l'esprit du tiki qui inspira à Disney l'idée des « Audio-Animatroniques » qui deviendraient le cœur de nombre d'attractions de Disneyland. Mais alors que le projet allait être conduit à terme, il s'avéra que la technologie futuriste des 225 robots, dirigés par une bande magnétique à quatorze canaux alimentant cent haut-parleurs et contrôlant 438 actions différentes, avait débordé largement l'espace du restaurant. Plutôt que de compromettre la complexité du spectacle, Walt résolut de supprimer le restaurant et d'en faire une attraction. Lorsque « Le Salon Tiki enchanté » ouvrit ses portes en 1963, le *New York Times* écrivit : « LA BANDE POLARIS AIDE L'ANIMATION DE DISNEY – De nouveaux procédés de synchronisation permettent aux totems de parler ... Dans le Salon Tiki enchanté, une profusion d'oiseaux artificiels colorés parlent, chantent ou sifflent. Des effigies de dieux païens jouent du tam-tam et chantent dans d'étranges langages. Des orages éclatent et les fontaines se mettent en marche. Des perroquets artificiels discourent en différents dialectes. »

Un compte-rendu exalté mais plutôt intellectuel, écrit par Don D. Jackson, M. D., professeur à Stanford et directeur du Palo Alto Mental Research Institute, comparait le Salon Tiki à d'autres lieux enchantés créés par l'homme : « JEU, PARADOXE ET FOULE : CRAINTE A DISNEYLAND ... C'est parce que je prétends avoir éprouvé en étant assis dans le Salon Tiki artificiel de Disneyland un aussi grand sentiment de crainte, d'émerveillement et de respect que dans quelques-unes des grandes cathédrales – Chartres, Reims et Notre-Dame.

Les bowlings furent également de la partie. Les bars adjacents, mais parfois aussi les établissements entiers, étaient généralement dédiés au dieu des loisirs. Le bowling était né dans les monastères allemands, où les moines demandaient aux fidèles de renverser un objet en forme de bouteille baptisé « Kegel » pour prouver leur dévotion. Le kegel de bois représentait le diable, et le renverser lavait le fidèle de ses péchés. On ignore si des quilles en forme de tiki ont jamais existé, mais dans de nombreux endroits, les chemises aloha et les chemises de bowling se mêlaient allègrement, tandis que les boissons tropicales calmaient les lancers des noceurs. L'un de ces endroits était le très sélect *Kapu Kai* (Mer interdite) à Rancho Cucamonga, une banlieue de Los Angeles. Quatre arches en A accueillaient les fervents disciples. Les tiki dressés entre les pistes et autour du bâtiment avaient été

sculptés par Milan Guanko. Les reliefs tiki de la porte d'entrée accueillaient avec un sourire les noceurs, mais ceux de l'intérieur adressaient une grimace à ceux qui s'en allaient. Des tapis tiki couvraient les sols et le Salon du Feu tahitien présentait d'impressionnantes peintures murales. Et pourtant, malgré son design remarquable, le *Kapu Kai* ne survécut pas à la fin du 20e siècle.

HÔTEL, MOTEL

Le tourisme et les tiki marchaient main dans la main dans l'Amérique des années 1960, et comme les enseignes des motels étaient les totems de la culture routière américaine, de nombreux établissements utilisèrent le tiki pour attirer l'attention. Phares dans la mer urbaine, leurs torches tiki en néon ou alimentées au gaz clignotaient pour les voyageurs épuisés et les négociants. La Polynésie était désormais accessible par la route. Le motel, une mutation américaine de l'hôtel, fut créée pour la vache sacrée à quatre roues, symbole du progrès et de la prospérité qu'est la voiture américaine des années 1950. A cette époque, il n'y avait d'autre limite que le ciel pour les constructeurs d'automobiles, les dimensions et les formes de leurs produits soutenant la comparaison avec les vaisseaux spatiaux. Ces aéroglisseurs avaient besoin de ports facilement accessibles où leurs pilotes puissent se reposer avant le prochain voyage. Afin de signaler ces ports de l'espace dans le vaste univers urbain, de gigantesques emblèmes rougeoyants furent érigés au bord des grandes artères de circulation. L'emblème du motel est un symbole classique de la culture américaine. Le fait que la ville d'Anaheim, patrie de Disneyland et qui attire les touristes du monde entier à la recherche de la culture pop américaine, ait détruit en 1998 la plupart des emblèmes tels celui du « Pitcairn », est donc un véritable « signe » d'ignorance. On a remarqué qu'une icône culturelle est particulièrement menacée de destruction juste avant que sa valeur soit redécouverte. Par conséquent, il faut s'attendre à ce que de mauvaises répliques de ces emblèmes soient érigés dans quelques années à Disneyland. L'emblème du *Hanalei* à San Diego est un parfait exemple « Avant » et « Après » d'ignorance commerciale où, au nom de la modernisation, que le banal caractère standard se substitue à l'expression individuelle. Tout comme l'emblème « Stardust » à Las Vegas, il a été remplacé par un banal caractère standard sans rapport avec le thème.

Les motels tiki ne fleurissent pas seulement dans les régions au climat doux, mais

également dans d'autres Etats américains. Le bâtiment principal du *Tiki Motor Inn* à Lake George, dans l'Etat de New York, était entouré de palmiers artificiels couverts verts sous la neige.

Toutefois la seule authentique chaîne de motels tiki est apparue dans les villes du désert californien : Ken Kimes dirigea jadis quarante motels dont cinq étaient ornés de tiki produits par les artisans de Oceanic Arts : il s'agissait du *Tropics* implanté à Indio, Blythe, Rosemead, Modesto et Palm Springs. Quatre d'entre eux présentent toujours des tiki qui ont bien survécu grâce au climat sec. Le *Tropics* de Palm Springs est le plus élaboré. Espérons que la redécouverte de Palm Springs comme centre du modernisme des années 1950 aidera à conserver ce précieux temple tiki.

SANS EGAL DANS LA VIE DU CELIBATAIRE

« Traversez la passerelle sculptée au-dessus du puits ardent de la déesse Pelé ; là où la lave est sur le point d'entrer en ébullition et la terre de trembler. Vous vous trouvez alors dans le meilleur des mondes, loin du stress, des ennuis et des soucis, mais à quelques minutes seulement des transports en commun, des églises et à quelques secondes de la terre ferme ... Dans ce décor fantastique, Pelé est tout. Elle a été et demeure dans le panthéon hawaïen. Vous vous détendrez et vous prélasserez au soleil au bord du bassin bordé de palmiers, dont l'eau, issue de la fontaine de corail, se déverse dans le splendide lagon. Sur la passerelle intérieure, vous vous retrouverez au milieu des ruines de son royaume, là où les vestiges de Hopoé et de Lohiau se sont transformés en deux grands rochers au sein des eaux tumultueuses qui s'écoulent sur la pente couverte de lave d'un volcan en éruption. Ici, réconforté par les dieux, vous pourrez trouver le repos du guerrier et vivre au milieu du magnifique décor de palmiers sans égal dans la vie du célibataire ... Prenez votre clé et devenez l'un des habitants de ce petit village exotique au centre d'une ville animée. »

Cet exemple évocateur de poésie pop polynésienne extrait de la brochure de la résidence *Pele* donne une idée du mal que se donnèrent les promoteurs pour créer ces établissements « polynésiens ». Les concepts architecturaux s'appuyaient sur les bars et les restaurants tiki, et dans le cas unique de la résidence *Pele*, on copia les caractères et les notes de pochette d'un célèbre album de musique exotique. Le même promoteur conçut un autre complexe d'appartements attrayant, *Shelter Isle*, mais la brochure publicitaire annonçait, vingt ans à l'avance, la décadence à venir : « Lorsque l'on quitte l'espace récréatif et que l'on flâne le long des chemins sinueux, on se trouve soudain au milieu des ruines d'un village indigène abandonné au bord d'un petit lac arrosé par des cascades descendant des parois couvertes de lave d'un volcan bouillonnant.

Lorsque l'archéologue urbain découvrit cette installation au milieu des années 1990, ne subsistait de ces « vestiges » que des rochers de lave noyés dans un bassin. Généralement, les villages tiki (ensembles résidentiels polynésiens) fournissent à l'archéologue un environnement plus gratifiant, car ils ont bien mieux survécu à l'abolition de l'idolâtrie que les temples tiki (restaurants et bars) qui leur ont donné jour. Moins soumis aux changements de goût que l'industrie de la restauration, ils représentent parfois des sanctuaires virtuels de ces espèces menacées que sont les tiki.

Même si certains propriétaires et gérants ont tenté de les mettre au goût du jour avec un zèle de missionnaire, et que de nombreux tiki se sont dégradés ou été volés par des pilleurs de sépultures, parcourir la mer urbaine de Los Angeles en quête de palmiers géants et de pignons en A peut toujours générer des découvertes spectaculaires. Au « Tahitian Village », dans la San Fernando Valley, les archétypes du feu et de l'eau sont représentés par deux sculptures indigènes à la Gauguin qui flanquent la passerelle de l'entrée. La figure masculine crachait autrefois de l'eau dans ses mains, qui à leur tour la déversaient dans le fossé, tandis qu'une flamme de gaz jaillissait de la main de la figure féminine. Un masque en ciment de 2,20 m de hauteur, des poteaux tiki et des lances croisées sur des boucliers en acier répartis tout autour sont quelques-unes des caractéristiques de ce complexe d'habitation.

Les torches tiki du « Polynesian Village » de Playa del Rey se sont éteintes, ainsi que les feux volcaniques qui avaient coutume de jaillir de la cascade principale. Mais les poutres extérieures sculptées, les jardins et l'architecture en lave/ciment d'Armet & Davis, demeurent de parfaits exemples d'un style qui s'est développé à une époque où l'on souhaitait en même temps « retourner à l'état sauvage » et vivre à proximité d'un aéroport. C'était une époque où les voyages en avion étaient chic et n'évoquaient pas le bruit, la pollution et le stress : « Les luxueux et élégants équipements aérodynamiques, reflets de l'âge du moteur à réaction, sont habilement mariés avec les couleurs, le roman-

tisme et le charme des îles des mers du Sud afin de créer un nouveau et délicieux mode de vie, à la résidence polynésienne de Playa del Rey … Les figures sculptées de vrais tiki veillent sur ces paysages splendides et luxuriants tout en promettant santé, bonheur et sérénité. »

Tout comme les temples, les villages étaient répandus dans toute la Californie mais, également comme eux, leur présence ne se limitait pas aux endroits les plus chauds. Tout le long de la West Coast, autour de Seattle, à Tacoma et Bremerton, ville de construction navale, on construisait de nombreux lotissements tiki. Partout en Amérique, des communautés plus ou moins organisées acclamaient l'effigie du dieu des loisirs. Les noms de ces îles de banlieue étaient aussi évocatrices que leurs styles. Du style « Beachcomber », « Asiatique », « Primitif », « Bambou » au style « Gros Samoa », ils représentaient tous les éléments de l'esthétique tiki. Certaines ailes ou parties de ces résidences avaient leurs propres désignations telles que « Port abrité » ou « Mauna Loa », empruntées à des sites hawaïens ou à des hôtels.

La Résidence *Exotic Isle* à Alhambra, dans la banlieue de Los Angeles, aujourd'hui essentiellement peuplée d'immigrés asiatiques, fut jusqu'à une date très récente une autre manifestation impressionnante de la foi tiki. Une salle de détente située au-dessus de la cascade centrale en constitue le centre et peut être considérée comme l'équivalent tiki de « Falling Water » de Frank Lloyd Wright.

LA POLYNESIE A SA PORTE

Par plus d'un côté, le désir de l'Américain moyen de « retourner à l'état sauvage » était une régression à l'enfance. Il était facile d'oublier les responsabilités du travail et de la famille lors des garden-parties « luau », un genre de fêtes d'anniversaire pour « les grands » où l'amusement et les jeux étaient de nouveau permis. On rêvetait des chemises hawaïennes fleuries et des « Muu Muus », on absorbait des aliments doux et on ingurgitait des breuvages encore plus doux qui ramenaient l'intellect à un état de conscience infantile. Les adultes blancs dansaient le houla et s'essayaient aux chants en langue hawaïenne : « Tous les KANES, VAHINES et KEIKIS (hommes, femmes et enfants) veulent WIKI WIKI (se précipiter) à un LUAU (fête) hawaïen. Les MALHINIS (nouveaux venus) veulent connaître la signification des mots étranges qu'ils entendent au cours du luau. Les femmes porteront des HOLOKUS (robes de princesses hawaïennes avec une traîne) ou des MUU MUUS (tuniques

flottantes à fleurs). Les Kanés portent des chemises ALOHA (chemises de sport hariolées). Aucun BADAPLE (chapeau) n'est requis. Les ALOHA (vœux) sont exprimés en plaçant un LEI (collier de fleurs) autour du cou du malihini. Le luau est servi sur de longues tables placées dans un LANAI (véranda ouverte) ou sous un baldaquin en feuilles de palmiers. La nourriture est cuisinée dans un IMU (four enfoui dans la terre) réalisé en creusant un LUA (trou) dans le sol, et en remplissant de POHAKU (cailloux) et de KUNI (petit bois). Un AHI (feu) est allumé pour chauffer les pohaku. Le PUA (cochon) cuisiné dans l'imu est un PUA KALUA. Si le luau est un AHAAINA (grande fête), il faudra des heures avant qu'il soit PAU (achevé) et que tout le monde rentre pour HIAMOE (dormir). Le sommeil vient vite car l'OPU (estomac) est satisfait après tant de KAU KAU (nourriture). »

On creusait des trous imu dans les jardins et les cours comme si la ruée vers l'or avait recommencé, mais le simple désir de retourner à l'état sauvage n'était pas suffisant. Il fallait un décor approprié. On pouvait trouver les éléments nécessaires à ces happenings dans des pépinières et des magasins spécialisés tels que « Sea and Jungle » dans la Valley, « Oceanic Arts » à Whittier, ou « Johnson Products » à Chicago. On pouvait y obtenir les torches tiki, les nattes en chanvre, les feuilles de palmiers, les poteaux de bambou, les filets de pêche, les lances et les tambours, et tout objet en forme de tiki. C'est ainsi que l'on construisit des huttes tiki dans les jardins et que des idoles furent érigées au bord des piscines et dans les patios, devenant ainsi les nouveaux nains de jardin de l'Amérique.

Le bricoleur adroit se voyait proposer des kits complets avec les instructions pour construire son propre bar tiki. Dans de nombreux logements de banlieue, les caves se transformèrent en salles de chahut, où les grandes personnes se rassemblaient pour des cocktails et des conversations « entre adultes ». Lorsque le bambou et le rotin perdirent de leurs attraits, on ajouta des bars tiki sculptés et des chaises de la maison Witco. Toujours à la pointe du bon goût, Elvis Presley équipa sa « Jungle Room » à Graceland avec du mobilier de chez Witco. Elvis surfait sur la crête de la vague polynésienne avec des films tels que « Blue Hawaii », « Paradise Hawaiian Style », et « Clambake », qui montre le meilleur luau jamais filmé sur une plage de Floride.

LES ARTISTES

Les créateurs de cette forme artistique qu'est le Moderne Tiki, les sculpteurs de tiki américains, n'ont jamais été acceptés comme des artistes. Si leurs productions étaient déclarées « authentiques », il ne fut jamais clairement affirmé qu'elles étaient originales. Personne ne voulait attirer l'attention sur le fait que le visage basané d'un sculpteur tel que Vince Buono, par exemple, provenait de ses origines italo-new-yorkaises et non des îles des mers du Sud. Le style tiki n'était pas une trahison intentionnelle, il répondait simplement au besoin du public de s'illusionner, s'entourant ainsi que ses créateurs d'un épais voile de mystère. La tronçonneuse de Leroy Schmalz, que l'on voit en pleine action, était proscrite dans les démonstrations de sculpture publiques, au cours desquelles on recourait au maillet et au ciseau. Ce chapitre voudrait donner à certains de ces artistes, choisis pour représenter tous ceux que nous ne pouvons citer, la reconnaissance qui leur est due.

Leroy Schmalz et Boob van Oosting fondèrent leur entreprise d'objets décoratifs « Oceanic Arts » à Whittier, dans la banlieue de Los Angeles, à la fin des années 1950, au plus chaud de la folie tiki. Après un démarrage modeste avec des amulettes tiki et des masques en feuilles de palmier, « Oceanic Arts » devint vite incontournable comme fabricant et fournisseur d'art et de matériel tiki du pays. La société décrocha des contrats avec toutes les chaînes importantes, de *Don the Beachcomber* à *Kon-Tiki*, et pratiquement tous les sculpteurs de cette industrie travaillèrent avec elles à un moment donné. Si les tiki étaient parfois dessinés par les architectes ou les décorateurs, la plupart du temps c'étaient les sculpteurs qui réalisaient leur propre vision et qui parfois concevaient l'ensemble de la décoration intérieure.

La liste des réalisations d'« Oceanic Arts » est considérable, puisque cette société a eu partie liée avec la plupart des temples tiki figurant dans ce livre. Du *Kahiki* dans l'Ohio, ou le *Mai Kai* en Floride, aux *The Tikis* du Monterey Park (chapitre 10), on retrouve des objets d'« Oceanic Arts » dans toute l'Amérique. Même le très respectable Bishop Museum de Honolulu expose, sinon dans ses vitrines, du moins sur les murs de sa cafétéria, certaines de leurs sculptures. Le phénomène de croisement culturel du style tiki atteignit son apogée lorsque les idoles manufacturées d'« Oceanic Arts » furent exportées dans des hôtels et des restaurants de Hawaii, de Samoa et de Tahiti. Aujourd'hui, « Oceanic Arts » est l'unique fournisseur de décors

polynésiens à avoir survécu avec succès à l'abolition du tiki, attirant une nouvelle génération d'explorateurs du monde entier sur les rivages de Whittier, Californie.

C'est de l'autre côté du Golden Gate Bridge, au nord de San Francisco, dans le pittoresque port de plaisance de Sausalito, que l'ex-marin Barney West installa son « Tiki Junction ». Il avait trouvé sa vocation au cours de la Seconde Guerre mondiale, alors qu'il était retenu dans les îles Marianne. Le logo du « Tiki Junction » fut trouvé dans un livre publié à l'occasion de la première exposition d'art des mers du Sud aux Etats-Unis, en 1946, livre qui inspira également le logo de Trader Vic. *Trader Vic* étant situé de l'autre côté de la baie, à Emeryville, près d'Oakland, il devint le principal client des tiki de Barney. On trouve encore certaines de ces effigies au style inimitable dans les établissements de la chaîne *Trader Vic*, à travers le monde. Barney jouait à la perfection le rôle du bohème cavaleur et buvant sec, et il a depuis longtemps rejoint le paradis du tiki.

PAGE 248

Milan Guanko apprit la sculpture auprès de son père, au cours de son enfance aux Philippines. Après avoir émigré aux Etats-Unis en 1928 et travaillé dans l'épicerie, il trouva son créneau lorsqu'apparut la folie polynésienne. Il devint finalement l'un des sculpteurs tiki les plus prolifiques et les plus influents des Etats-Unis, son style étant copié et commercialisé pour répondre à la demande croissante des noceurs tiki. Au nombre de ses créations figurent notamment *The Islands* à Phoenix, Arizona, le *Kapu Kai* à Rancho Cucamonga, et le *Polynesian Village* de Ren Clark à Fort Worth, Texas, pour lequel Guanko et deux sculpteurs mexicains, Juan Razo et Fidel Rodriguez (qui avaient équipé le *Mauna Loa* à Mexico), sculptèrent plus de deux cents tiki, les uns en tabourets de bar, d'autres en géants de 3,5 mètres de haut. Exemple du paradis de l'art polynésien en 1960, rien n'a subsisté de cette forêt virtuelle de tiki, et l'on ignore où se trouvent la plupart des ses habitants.

Dans l'univers de Witco de William Westernhaver, un bon morceau de bois était un morceau de bois sculpté. Qu'il s'agisse de ses tableaux faits de « reliefs en bois brûlé sur tapis épais » ou de ces ensembles complets pour « chambre à coucher primitive », aucune surface lisse n'échappait à la tronçonneuse de ce fou. Partout où il pouvait tailler un visage de tiki, les copeaux s'envolaient. Le bois était ensuite brûlé au chalumeau afin de faire apparaître sa texture et d'épaisses veines noires. Il n'y avait pas que de l'art polynésien, les décors modernes et de style

conquistador étaient également produits en série dans la fabrique de Witco à Seattle. On peut encore voir les travaux de Westernhaver dans des motels de Floride et dans des magasins d'articles d'occasion dans tous les Etats-Unis, Witco ayant eu à une époque des salles d'exposition à Chicago, Dallas, Denver et Seattle. Sur la liste de ses clients figuraient Elvis Presley, Hugh Hefner et même, à ce qu'on dit, certaines « maisons de mauvaise réputation ». Parmi ses œuvres les plus remarquables, on note une grande variété de bars et de fontaines tiki.

L'auteur de ces lignes prépare actuellement une monographie consacrée à l'œuvre prolifique de cet original. Enfin, il désirerait exprimer son espoir que le présent ouvrage pourra contribuer à ce que la culture tiki retrouve auprès du public l'attention qui lui est due.

CREDITS

The publishers wish to thank the copyright holders who greatly assisted in this publication. Every effort was made to identify and contact individual copyright holders; omissions are unintentional. The following are credits for copyrighted material: all illustrations not mentioned here are from the collection of the author.

Armet & Davis, Los Angeles (CA): 24, 58 /59, 148 ; Bamboo Ben Archives, Huntington Beach (CA): 64 ; Forde Photographers, Seattle (WA): 71 ; House Industries, Wilmington (DE): 121,51; Ulli Maier, Düsseldorf: 162 top; Fred Milkie Photographers, Seattle (WA): 79 bottom; Pete Moruzzi, Los Angeles (CA): 9 bottom; Oceanic Arts, Whittier: 159, 160, Rautenstrauch-Joest-Museum für Völkerkunde, Cologne: 8, 9 top, 48/49 top left; Rue des Archives / Brierre, Paris: 22 bottom; San Francisco Library, San Francisco (CA): 38 top left; S.S Archives Shooting Star, Hollywood (CA): 123 top; © 1962 Walt Disney Productions: 132, 133 bottom, 156 top

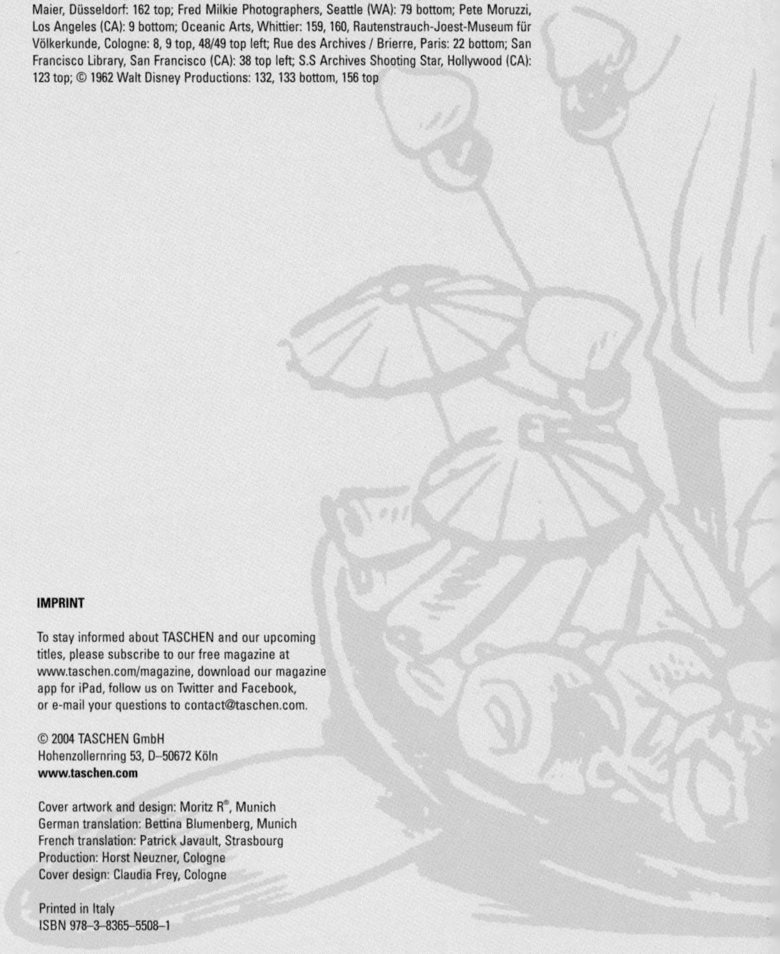

IMPRINT

To stay informed about TASCHEN and our upcoming titles, please subscribe to our free magazine at www.taschen.com/magazine, download our magazine app for iPad, follow us on Twitter and Facebook, or e-mail your questions to contact@taschen.com.

© 2004 TASCHEN GmbH
Hohenzollernring 53, D–50672 Köln
www.taschen.com

Cover artwork and design: Moritz R®, Munich
German translation: Bettina Blumenberg, Munich
French translation: Patrick Javault, Strasbourg
Production: Horst Neuzner, Cologne
Cover design: Claudia Frey, Cologne

Printed in Italy
ISBN 978–3–8365–5508–1

COLLECTABLES
AND
BOOKS

An·tiki